Regenerating Schools

Also available from Network Continuum

Schools and Communities – John West-Burnham, Maggie Farrar and George Otero
Personalizing Learning – John West-Burnham and Max Coates
Learn to Transform – David Crossley and Graham Corbyn
Leading Change in Schools – Sian Case
Understanding Systems Leadership – Pat Collarbone and John West-Burnham
The Constant Leader – Max Coates

Regenerating Schools

Leading the transformation of standards and services through community engagement

Malcolm Groves

with John Baumber

and Gabrielle Leigh, Dee Pullen, Bill Temple, Sheila Yates

network
continuum

Continuum International Publishing Group
Network Continuum

The Tower Building   80 Maiden Lane
11 York Road   Suite 704
SE1 7NX   New York NY 10038

www.networkcontinuum.co.uk
www.continuumbooks.com

British Library Cataloguing-in-Publication Data
A catalogue record for this book is available from the British Library.

ISBN: 9781855394575 (paperback)

Library of Congress Cataloguing-in-Publication Data
Groves, Malcolm.
Regenerating schools : leading transformation of standards and
services in secondary schools through community engagement / Malcolm
Groves ; with John Baumber . . . [et al.].
    p. cm.
    Includes bibliographical references and index.
    ISBN 978-1-85539-457-5
    1. School management and organization–Case studies. 2. Community and school–Case studies.
3. Education, Secondary–Case studies. 4. Educational leadership–Case studies. I. Baumber,
John. II. Title.

LB2806.G76 2008
371.19—dc22

                                        2008021935

Typeset by Newgen Imaging Systems Pvt Ltd, Chennai, India
Printed and bound in Great Britain by Cromwell Press, Wiltshire

Contents

Foreword

Brian J. Caldwell

Managing Director, Educational Transformations Pty Ltd
Professorial Fellow, University of Melbourne (Dean of Education 1998–2004)
Associate Director (Global), International Networking
for Educational Transformation (iNet)

What is the best way to learn about the successful transformation of schools and then disseminate the findings so that all can achieve the same success? We are in a period of time when the best way to get started is to provide rich accounts of how particular schools have gone about it and then choose one or more strategies to spread the word. Such strategies include site visits, seminars, workshops, master classes led by those who have played a key role, and publications, including books, that are written in a style that cuts through to the practitioner. *Regenerating Schools* models this last 'best way' and provides an accessible analysis that is a sure guide to others. In this instance, the focus is on an important factor in transformation, namely, community engagement.

As far as research methodology is concerned, we are in a period of time when the case study, or change study as it is described in *Regenerating Schools*, has come into its own, complementing in a more significant way than in the recent past the survey style of investigation. It is time for concepts and theories to catch up with the best practice of transformation. It is still early days, so the more we can capture the richness and complexity of the process, the sooner we can move on to theory building. *Regenerating Schools* makes an important contribution.

We have followed a similar approach in our work at Educational Transformations, building on earlier work for the International Networking for Educational Transformation (iNet) project of the Specialist Schools and Academies Trust. Our starting point was to revisit the concept of the self-managing school, for we sensed that the best practice of self-management had outstripped the initial concept as we described it in our earlier work more than two decades ago. We then broadened our investigation to consider the way schools were moving towards transformation, defined as significant, systematic and sustained change that secures success for all students in all settings. Over 3 years we conducted case studies (49), master classes (4) and workshops (60) involving school and school system leaders in 11 countries. Forty of the case studies were contributed by school leaders in 13 of the 60 workshops. Several workshops were incorporated in conferences and post-graduate programmes in leadership and management.

An initial model of the findings was constructed and published in *Re-imagining Educational Leadership* (Caldwell 2006).[1] A refined model was published in *Raising the Stakes: from Improvement to Transformation in the Reform of Schools* (Caldwell and Spinks 2008).[2] Our work did not stop there and the model was then tested in deep case studies of five secondary schools in each of six countries (Australia, China, England, Finland, US and Wales) in a project jointly funded by the Australian Government and Welsh Assembly Government.

The model provides a powerful framework for what is described in *Regenerating Schools*. Let me explain why. We found that transformation calls for strengthening and aligning four kinds of capital, namely, intellectual capital, social capital, spiritual capital and financial capital. To build this strength and secure such alignment requires outstanding leadership and governance.

Intellectual capital is the level of knowledge and skill of those who work in or for the school. Social capital is the strength of formal and informal partnerships and networks involving the school, parents, community, business and industry, indeed, all individuals, agencies, organizations and institutions that have the potential to support and, where appropriate, be supported by the school. Spiritual capital is the strength of moral purpose and the degree of coherence among values, beliefs and attitudes about life and learning. For some schools, spiritual capital has a foundation in religion. In other schools, spiritual capital may refer to ethics and values shared by members of the school and its community. Financial capital is the money available to support the school. Governance is the process through which the school builds its intellectual, social, financial and spiritual capital and aligns them to achieve its goals.

We identified 10 sample indicators for each form of capital and for governance – a total of 50 indicators – and 40 of these were evident in each of the 30 case study schools in the international project and the remaining 10 were evident in at least one school.

Regenerating Schools provides the most powerful account we have yet read of a critical aspect of social capital – community engagement – and highlights how the energy must flow in two directions – from the school to community and from the community to school. It also provides a remarkable illustration of how community engagement is a potent way to build the other three forms of capital. Each of the ten sample indicators of strong social capital that were validated in the international project is evident in the case studies in *Regenerating Schools*. We therefore sense a synergy in our joint international endeavours.

Let's look more closely at what has been reported in the pages that follow. The uplifting first section (Imagine . . .) makes clear that this book is about transformation – regeneration is a particular kind of transformation. It invites us to imagine schools that allow total flexibility in curriculum and pedagogy, that constitute twenty-first-century learning communities based on new forms of ownership and delivery, and that are leading-edge enterprises and beacons of hope in highly disadvantaged settings. It sets out to show the realization of imagination.

There is something special about the approach in this book, which avoids the pitfalls in the publication of case studies. One pitfall is to simply present a series of cases and then leave it to readers to draw conclusions and settle on strategies to suit their settings. Some authors and editors go a little further and assist the reader by providing a synthesis. This may be helpful but a synthesis can wring the life out of the story. Some reports of survey-based research do the same. Not so this book; these pitfalls have been avoided by adopting an approach that will be appreciated by scholars, policymakers and practitioners. Each of the main parts of this book has two elements. One is an extended reflection on a theme; the other contains the case ('change study') that illustrates the theme in a particular national setting. The themes taken together describe the process of transformation in general, and regeneration in particular – imagine, understand, plan, build, lead, transform – and these parts of this book would each make a worthy publication in their own right. Add the case study and impact is powerful.

Brief reference is made here to the three international cases given, for they illustrate the breathtaking scope of this book. Consider the first case of the Kunskapsskolan in Sweden, which is not one school but 29 schools that provide for 15 per cent of secondary provision in that country. It is a blend of several of the famous OECD scenarios on the future of schools described in Understand . . . (Section 2 of *Regenerating Schools*). There is superb use of technology, the teacher's role as a professional is heightened, learning is personalized and there is significant engagement of the community. New approaches to ownership, leadership, governance and architecture are illustrated.

Consider the case of Caroline Springs College in Australia. It is counter-intuitive because it deals with a school – actually several schools that make up a single college that have been created on green-field sites over the last decade – rather than a now successful school that has been regenerated from one that was struggling. In this case, the college was created as an integral part of a new community. It is a breathtaking example of how new structures and processes can be created in a system of public education in which traditional arrangements were seen by many as immutable; for example, traditional boundaries between primary and secondary schools and teacher-centred learning. Boundaries are blurred, and student voice is a powerful vector.

The most uplifting case is surely the last: Banareng Primary School in Atteridgeville in the Republic of South Africa. The authors acknowledge the plight of the school before a transforming principal took charge: 'a depressingly impoverished and dysfunctional school'. The school was transformed. Every kind of capital – intellectual, social, spiritual, financial – was strengthened and aligned through outstanding leadership and governance. The same principles that underpinned the regeneration of schools in other countries are evident at Banareng. There can be no excuse for schools in every setting to not achieve what was achieved in a setting that is at first sight impossibly difficult to transform.

Outstanding governance was critical in each of the six case studies, but who was involved and what their roles and responsibilities were differed from case to case. Indeed, if account is taken of the other examples embedded in the extended reflections that accompany these cases, it can be concluded that there is no one best way to govern a school. This reinforces the view we have formed at Educational Transformations and it is why we have defined governance as the process through which the school builds its intellectual, social, financial and spiritual capital and aligns them to achieve its goals. There has been a preoccupation with structures and specifying roles and responsibilities. These are important, indeed they are necessary, but the focus must shift to the purpose of governance, as our definition does, and this opens up the possibility that there are myriad ways to do it.

We now recognize that leadership and governance go hand in hand. There cannot be good governance without good leadership. Every example in *Regenerating Schools* demonstrates that change on the scale of transformation does not occur without outstanding leadership, certainly including the headteacher or principal, but also on the part of many others, within the school and across the wider community of interests that support or are supported by the school.

A consequence is that professional development programmes for leaders in the school community must deal with community engagement and an exemplary programme, offered by the Specialist Schools and Academies Trust (SSAT), is the starting point of *Regenerating Schools*. There is reinforcement here of an important sub-theme that runs through this book, namely, that schools cannot be transformed if they are acting alone.

At first sight, this book is an account of how schools can be regenerated through community engagement. It accomplishes this purpose. More fundamentally, however, it is a book about the regeneration of the concept of schools, for it describes and illustrates change to every element of school design. It accomplishes this deeper purpose in a manner that demands the attention of policymakers and practitioners around the world. It is an audacious book that not only gives hope that transformation is possible but engenders optimism that it can be achieved.

Malcolm Groves is not afraid to enter the debate on contentious issues. This is particularly evident when he writes on the theme of leadership. The context is England and the creation of new kinds of schools such as academies. Tensions in matters of governance and re-engineering the workforce are acknowledged. Strong positions are taken. It is a brave book as well as an audacious book.

Malcolm and his associates take seriously the adage in the final chapter: 'set the controls for the heart of the sun' but they recognize that oblivion is certain if another is not honoured: 'grow trust like there *is* a tomorrow'. Is it possible to achieve on a large scale what is promised in *Regenerating Schools* but illustrated by barely a handful? You bet! Read on!

Author's acknowledgements

This book would not have been possible without the visionary support of the Specialist Schools and Academies Trust, and in particular Mike Goodfellow, in commissioning and promoting a leadership programme to help senior school leaders better understand community engagement and its impact for their school's future.

In developing that programme for the Trust, I have been privileged to work with an extraordinary group of headteachers who have helped to shape the ideas behind it and to facilitate the learning of others through the depth and insight of their experience. All of these have made direct contributions to this book.

In particular, John Baumber has provided enormous support in the writing of this book, including contributing two of the change studies and some chapters in Sections 2, 4 and 5.

I am also especially grateful to Steve Baker, Tony Cooper, Clive Corbett, Ian Mowbray and Alan Stevens, all from that group, who have all willingly provided vital and direct help with content, advice and enthusiasm, and to Sheila Yates for contributing one of the change studies as well.

A range of other people has also made significant contributions. Brian Caldwell, Bella Irlicht, Gabrielle Leigh, Dee Pullen and Bill Temple, all responded with enormous enthusiasm, despite very busy lives, to really help open up a fresh international dimension to the book's thinking. And I am indebted to Peter Barnes, Stephen Forster, Hugh Howe, Mohammed Mehmet, Sefika Mertkan-Ozunlu, Jan Stoney and Ian Wigston, who have each willingly contributed time, ideas or material for key sections. Jane Buckley, Steve Gallaher, Richard Gerver, Caroline Humphreys, Lesley and Michael James, Julie Richards, Graham Silverthorne and Chris Tomsett have all read and commented helpfully on ideas or text at various stages. And Susan Potter has provided invaluable support in preparing and formatting the various drafts of the final manuscript.

To all, I offer my sincere thanks. I hope this finished work does justice to the confidence and contribution they have all so willingly offered, and to the vision and optimism so clearly exemplified in their schools.

Malcolm Groves
February 2008

Introduction

At the core of the thinking behind this book is the belief that, under the conditions that currently prevail, schools acting alone and without real engagement with their communities cannot achieve the greatest possible improvement and transformation in learning. As a result, they will fail to equip their students adequately for the world in which they will live and work.

There is an increasing awareness in both academic and policy circles that high social capital enhances academic success. Therefore, one answer to academic underachievement is not just to strive incrementally to improve the efficiency of schools themselves, but rather to focus also on increasing the social capital within their community. If educational success is, in part, a function of high social capital, then educational leadership has to make the development of social capital a high priority.

This book has grown directly from and builds on the experience of developing and running a 2-year leadership development programme for English secondary school leaders on behalf of the Specialist Schools and Academies Trust (SSAT), as well as substantial career experience in developing, leading, supporting and inspecting schools and their community dimension.

Over 200 school leaders have now passed through the SSAT leadership programme 'Specialist Schools and their Communities: Developing Innovative Leadership for the Future'[3] – over 5 per cent of English secondary schools in just 18 months at the time of writing. This scale of interest in a relatively short period of time is in itself some indication of the potential appetite among school leaders for fresh approaches and fresh thinking around the national schools agenda, in ways which link creatively the raising of standards, future visioning and community engagement, and address the implications of all that for school leadership.

This moves beyond present understandings of the community role of, for example, specialist schools in England, who currently comprise over 90 per cent of secondary schools in the country and form the locus for many current government aspirations for both school and community improvement. In addition to a prime focus on raising standards, there has been strong emphasis within the specialist schools programme on providing targeted learning opportunities for the local community, including other local school primary and secondary schools as well as specific targeted groups within the community. The added value here lies in the learning outcomes for these groups within the community. But there is, as well, an often unrecognized potential for a real dividend for the school itself.

The shift now needed is for a step-change in emphasis from the school as an institution with a sole focus on institutional improvement to the school as an agency able to lead community transformation. By focusing on and improving community interaction, schools can begin making a significant contribution to developing the entire community's capacity to learn, including, very most importantly, those for whom it has a statutory responsibility.

The purpose of this book is to explore what these ideas might mean in practice, how those benefits could be achieved without losing focus on the need to raise attainment for all, and what the implications are for school leaders now and in the future. Central to this understanding is a concept of schools as agents of regeneration, both for themselves and for their communities.

Section 1
Imagine . . .

IMAGINE being able to create a school that allows total flexibility over what is learned and how and when it is taught . . .

IMAGINE a school which realizes that for the long term the benefits of collaboration far outweigh the short-term gains of competition . . .

IMAGINE a twenty-first-century learning community, based on new forms of ownership and structures for delivery, committed to building a culture of lifelong learning . . .

IMAGINE being able to spend 2 years in planning and building a state-of-the-art new school for the twenty-first century that reflects a community-oriented mission . . .

IMAGINE developing and sustaining over time a leading-edge school in a new housing area surrounded by motorways which had little formal or planned community facilities and, among the population, low self esteem and little educational expectation . . .

IMAGINE developing a school that becomes a pioneer and a beacon when most children have not eaten a meal since the last time they came to school . . .

All these imaginings and more are explored in this book. Each represents a real school, three in England, three in other countries. Each of these schools has moved from imagination to reality, and success, in their own context, because they have understood and acted on some key messages about the relationship between schools and their communities.

Through that hard-won experience, and the underlying tested principles in which it is grounded, they can point the way for others who wish to transform standards and services for children and young people in their schools by understanding, then planning, building and leading that transformation.

1   What to say about us?

Future generations will remember ours as the age of . . . well, what, exactly? In particular, what will they say of the schools we have created in the late twentieth and early twenty-first century, when they look back on this time a century hence. Or even more importantly, since it is of only limited value trying to second guess the opinions of others as yet unborn, what would we really want them to say? Are we satisfied with what we have, or do we urgently need to re-imagine what we want from and for our schools, and our secondary schools in particular?

This book begins with an assumption – that there is only one possible answer to that question. A potent mix of economic, environmental, and social and moral considerations drives a compelling need for change. This new triple bottom line of school accountability reflects the changing nature of the globalized twenty-first-century world for which schools seek to prepare young people. There are though, as we shall see, powerfully competing visions of where that affirmation of the need for change might lead.

Drawing on experience of English secondary schools in particular, but also schools in other sectors and in other countries, this book is about how we both need, and can make, a particular step-change in the slow moves many schools have already started, away from being narrow focused, largely inward-facing organizations to becoming outgoing community centres of learning.

Schools need to do this now and with considered urgency if they are to

- contribute to the development of the future skills base of the country's needs for its long-term economic well being
- justify the significant public investment they receive
- use their position as a key, and sometimes only, significant social institution, but also one that does exist in every community, to act as an agency for cohesion and renewal

A school which is able to do all that we will call – for shorthand purposes only, as there is more than enough jargon flying around – a regenerating school. That not altogether elegant phrase does, nevertheless, capture the effect such a school has on all those whom it touches, as well as highlighting how the idea of school itself is in need of regeneration. We know there are already strong examples of such schools, and a number feature throughout this book, sharing their stories and experience, as well as providing studies in how change can happen and the impact it can have.

2　Beyond the island

What follows is not an account of a regenerating school. Instead, through a clear image, it describes schools that are quite the opposite. This account comes from America in the 1940s. But it is so close to many people's recent, or even current, experience that few who read it are unable to find echoes of real schools in the here and now:

> Many schools are like islands, set apart from the mainland of life by a deep moat of convention and tradition. A drawbridge is lowered at certain points of the day in order that the part-time inhabitants may cross over to the island in the morning and back to the mainland at night.
>
> Why do these young people go out to the islands? To learn how to live on the mainland. When they reach the island they are provided with excellent books that tell about life on the mainland.
>
> Once in a while as a special treat a bus takes a few of the young people off the island during the day to look at what happens on the mainland.
>
> When everyone on the island has left in the afternoon, the drawbridge is raised. Janitors clean up the island and the lights go out. No-one is left except perhaps a watchman keeping a vigil along the shoreline. The island is lifeless.
>
> Once a year people from the mainland visit the island to watch graduation, after which some islanders depart never to set foot on the island again. After graduates leave the island for the last time, they are bombarded by problems of life on the mainland. Occasionally one of them can be heard to say to another: 'I remember reading something about that when we were on the island'.[4]

The message of this book is clear. We can no longer afford islands, if we ever could.

3 The success and stalling of school improvement

But it is not as if schools have exactly been standing still in recent years. The rate of change in the overwhelming majority of schools has been huge, particularly over the last decade. In England, for a mix of reasons, most of them good, we have as a country and as an education service, devoted significant resources and immense effort over that period to school improvement and to what we have been pleased to call 'the standards agenda'. And there have been real gains as a result.

The school improvement movement has encouraged us to raise our expectations, to be less willing to settle for second or even third best, and to challenge the self-fulfilling prophecies of local determinism. It has been right to insist that local circumstance is not an excuse for failure and to highlight the extent to which young people in similar difficult circumstances can achieve very differently according to the school they attend. The standards agenda has given us, at least at one level, a clarity of expected outcome and a means to measure, compare and contrast. Targets have focused our attention on certain specifics and rewarded the achievement of these, as well as punishing failure to meet them. Being human, we have mostly risen to the challenge. Countless teachers and school leaders have worked unbelievably hard, and managed, with great striving, overall to make steady incremental improvement against those chosen measures.

It is a significant achievement that English secondary schools in the first years of the twenty-first-century work as well as they do, that attendance is so high, that bad behaviour isn't more widespread and that well over half of young people emerge with five good GCSE grades at the age of 16 years.

But there are signs, equally, of some cracks appearing, and progress stalling at the same time. A significant minority fail to secure qualifications, and this results in the UK having one of the worst 17+ education and training participation records among the Organization for Economic Co-operation and Development (OECD) countries. Equally serious, even though more young people are gaining five GCSE A*–C grades, too many of them leave school with only the faintest idea about how the world works and how to make a living, as employers often and loudly complain.[5]

That divide between the world of schools and the world of work has been an endemic feature of English education for generations. But is it an effect, or a cause, of the difficulties schools are experiencing in making progress at a faster rate with the standards agenda?

David Hopkins in a pamphlet for the SSAT, 'Every School a Great School',[6] describes and illustrates the plateau effect we seem to have reached in terms of English educational achievement and that is being experienced at all key stages. He sees it as an inevitable result of centrally driven change. He argues that the problem flows from a failure, during the 1997 Labour Government's first term, to think through how to build capacity for sustained improvement, and from the lack of the government having an overarching strategy for large-scale educational reforms. Such a strategy, he argues, now faces five challenges. There is:

- underperformance at all levels
- slow progress in secondary education
- too much focus on management rather than leadership
- a sense of the restricted nature of teaching quality
- limited understanding of the interrelationship of excellence and equity, with deprivation being the root cause of low attainment

That is not to say further incremental progress on standards is impossible or undesirable. Far from it. And Hopkins goes on to suggest cogently what is needed to bring that ongoing improvement about. However, such improvement against traditional assessment measures, though necessary, is not of itself sufficient to meet the needs of either young people or the economy. We need to broaden our understanding of purpose as well. And a significant part of that is about re-imagining and transforming the relationship between school and life and between schools and their communities.

One part of the explanation why this is so is well stated by what some may see as an unlikely champion. The Audit Commission in their 2006 report 'More than the Sum'[7] note that:

> School improvement and renewal are inseparable issues from neighbourhood improvement and renewal, particularly in the most disadvantaged areas. While schools are profoundly affected by their neighbourhoods, they equally have a key role in promoting cohesion and building social capital, for example by taking part in local regeneration schemes, offering adult education and helping families to access other local public services, such as health and childcare.

The report continues:

The strong relationship between parental socio-economic circumstances and pupil attainment is longstanding, and clear at both school and pupil level. More deprived pupils, and schools with more deprived intakes, generally perform less well academically than more affluent ones, across all Key Stages. However, statistical trends indicate that in recent years there has been some narrowing of the attainment gap at school level, although at pupil level less progress has been made. This suggests that issues associated with local socio-economic circumstances are still acting as a brake on improvement.

School and community regeneration are inextricably intertwined.

4   Shift happens

In 2007, despite the improvements made in the previous decade, the UK found itself slipping down international rankings,[8] and it has been the cause of not a little soul searching among all with an interest in schools. But there is an even more fundamental problem that is much less talked about. Doing well against our current narrow range of measures may not be enough. Because the world is changing – fast. One of the best ways to find out just how fast is to download a video from Youtube.

'Did You Know?' was put together by two American teachers Karl Fisch and Scott Macleod.[9] It originally started out as a PowerPoint presentation for a faculty meeting at Arapahoe High School in Centennial, Colorado, US, in August 2006. The presentation 'went viral' on the Web and, as of June 2007, had been seen by at least 5 million online viewers. Here are just a few of its indicators of change:

- It is estimated that a week's worth of **New York Times** contains more information than a person was likely to come across in a **lifetime** in the eighteenth century.
- It is estimated that 40 exabytes (that is 4.0×10^{19}) of unique new information will be generated worldwide this year. That's estimated to be more than in the previous 5,000 years.
- The amount of new technical information is doubling every 2 years. It is predicted to double every 72 hours by 2010.
- By 2023, a US$1,000 computer will exceed the computation capability of the Human Brain.
- Predictions are that by 2049, a US$1,000 computer will exceed the computational capabilities of the **human race**.

If even a fraction of that were to be true, we are living in – and educating for – times of exponential change.

Thomas Friedman, in his book '*The World is Flat*',[10] summarizes the new need for a broader educational purpose to reflect this new world. Looking from an economic perspective, albeit largely an American one, he suggests a new education formula, CQ + PQ > IQ, where C stands for curiosity and P stands for passion and IQ represents our traditional quotient of intelligence. Together these two attributes of curiosity and passion, he argues, carry more worth than any standard intelligence quotient (or 'pure' academic ability) in the new flat world facing all countries and their economies, a world driven by technological change, high-speed communication and globalization. IQ still matters in this flatter world, but creativity and passion matter even more. If that is true, then the message is not just confined to America.

What are we in Britain doing to educate towards that end? The successful application of Friedman's formula, matched to the insights of the Audit Commission, involves linking the island with the mainland in new and multiple ways. That has happened in rare instances in the past. It is beginning to happen more often and with more understanding, as the change studies throughout this book illustrate. But this is something all schools now need to learn – fast.

5 Digital world – analogue school

Meanwhile, what do young people themselves say of the enormous efforts we have been making on their behalf? Are they flattered? Grateful? How many ask, along with this young person, the troubling question 'why?'

Why do I get taught at the speed of other pupils?
Why do I take exams in the summer?
Why am I forced to fail exams this year when I could pass them next?
Why do I learn a foreign language alongside others who can't speak it?
Why do I have to watch a teacher struggle to use yesterday's technology?
Why do I have to memorize stuff I can look up on my mobile phone?
Why is there only one timetable when there are millions of individually customized Yahoos!?
Why are there so few subjects when I have hundreds of TV channels?
Why am I taught separate subjects when life is integrated?
Why do I have to write at school when everyone types in life?
Why do I have to accept a bad teacher when I never accept a bad burger?
Why is school analogue and grey when life is digital and technicolour?[11]

In other words, the world of school is far too often out of step with the world that very many young people experience, live and often work in, on a daily basis. Many of them will tolerate that discontinuity as the price to be paid for growing up and getting a foot on the ladder. But mere tolerance is not going to raise PQ and CQ. And numbers will inevitably switch off, with their minds, with their physical presence or with both, all curiosity and passion lost.

So, let's try turning the perspective around. As one headteacher asked: 'What would we need to do to make school as attractive to our young people as Disneyland?'

6   Learning for real

Just imagine! What would it take to make that possible? What would we need to stop doing? What would we need to do differently? What would we need to start doing?

Richard Gerver's answer came from the desire to create a contextual curriculum that enables children to see a practical purpose for their learning, while defining the concepts of citizenship, teamwork and opportunity:

> Our aim is that all children should leave Grange as independent learners aware of how key learning can support their future life choices.[12]

Grange is a fairly large primary school (430 children including a nursery) on the borders of Derbyshire and Nottinghamshire. It is an urban primary school housed in the 1940s purpose-built accommodation. The catchment is an interesting socio-economic mix ranging from professional to socially deprived families. It does not have a high ethnic mix.

'As educators', says Richard Gerver, 'we need to rethink approaches to teaching, realise that we have important "products", and find ways to convince our pupils that they need them. If they want to learn, they will, but we have to make it personal to each of them. Part of that is letting them help design their curriculum'.

'Teachers need to be like advertising executives', he goes on. 'We have to sell learning to pupils'.

So Richard and his staff decided to create an environment, a town. 'Grangeton' was born in 2002. The town inside the school is entirely run by children and includes a school council that acts in the way a town council does. There is an elected mayor who carries out ceremonial, as well as democratic, responsibilities. From the council stems the town's enterprises: there is a café and the team who run it are trained in food hygiene, marketing and customer relations. The language in use is French; children wanting to use the café must order food in French. The school shop is ultra-competitive and runs at a profit. The museum has the school's archives, and the media centre has a radio station, television studio and a journalism group. The writers have complete editorial control.

Initially, Grangeton was a Friday afternoon project but then it extended to run 5 days a week and became part of the fabric of the school. Teaching children to learn and live is the priority, and the nature of the project means that they can use their learning in a context. Pupils have roles in the town and they have to negotiate with their teachers to gain the time to do some of the town work.

What is significant is that this change of focus has enabled the school to raise attainment and achievement. Since introducing this new, personalized curriculum, Grange Primary School results have doubled in achievement, and the school has gone from below average to 'outstanding' within 3 years.

7 There are three R's in regeneration

Of course some would question whether the aspiration to be as popular as Disneyland was in any way a desirable end, even for a primary school like Grange. Schools, secondary schools, in particular, have to be more serious than that. Their aim, the purpose of schooling, is not enjoyment but learning, learning that will equip a young person with the skills society needs them to have if it is to secure the future well-being of its population.

There is though a major problem with that argument in the world we now inhabit. We no longer know what those skills are in any precise way, because most of the jobs for which we are endeavouring to prepare this generation of young people haven't yet been invented. According to former US Secretary of Education Richard Riley, the top 10 in-demand jobs, as they will be in 2010, did not exist in 2004.[13] And anyway simply replicating past models of economic development is not going to work if the planet is to have a sustainable future.

But the critique of a lack of seriousness could nonetheless hold an element of truth. Life is not just fun. It is at times serious, painful, hard and uncomfortable. Preparation for life needs to include the hurt as well as the fun. And the young will inherit particularly challenging economic and social problems to solve from the generation of us who have gone before.

> It is as if having extended babyhood through years undreamed of by previous generations, we have devised compulsory education to cope with the babysitting.[14]

Those words, written by a distinguished and pioneering public school headmaster, L. C. Taylor, nearly 40 years ago, still resonate today, perhaps more so in an increasingly risk-averse society and one which is now legislating to raise the statutory school-leaving age to 18 years, but not yet thinking coherently about what it wants to achieve from that extra time.

Taylor, in a very different context and from a very different background to Richard Gerver, went on to argue for the provision of real-life challenges for young people of secondary school age trapped in that peculiarly modern limbo of adolescence. In effect he began to develop a curriculum that gave young people an additional three R's, although this is my paraphrase of his thinking. It means offering:

- role – being taken seriously and carrying real responsibility for yourself and others
- risk – learning through doing, sometimes through failing
- reality – engaging with the real world including its problems and being expected to contribute

Through that thinking, he went on to establish a series of, for their day, ground-breaking initiatives to challenge the separation of school from the real world, and adolescence from life. Among his experiments at Sevenoaks School in Kent were the establishment of a Technical Activities Centre, 'to test and develop qualities which are all-important in science and technology but which do not always show up in examination results' and a Voluntary Service Unit 'to help give boys' (his was an all boys school at the time), 'an understanding of the society they live in and give the sort of boy who asks ghastly questions about purpose the experience of being useful'.

Not withstanding how much we have since learnt about how better to understand and take such ideas forward in the very different world of state schooling, these were prescient challenges to educational and social orthodoxy. In them lie the seeds of regeneration. They contain those three R's.

But the challenge today still remains for us to imagine a model of schooling that moves beyond what we have, with classrooms today, as well as what happens in them, often somewhat bizarrely unchanged in their fundamentals from those of 100 years ago. This is despite all our recently acquired knowledge of areas such as brain science and emotional intelligence, which has transformed our understanding of human learning, and most of which has come about in the last 15–20 years. It is despite the very different nature of the world we know our young people are growing up in, and in which they already live and frequently work and will need to do so for a good while to come.

In short, then, our challenge is this. Can we imagine a regenerating school? A school, that is, which consciously and coherently:

- connects schooling directly to real-world experience, including the involvement of a wide range of people sharing their knowledge, ideas and skills and acting as co-educators.
- contributes to increased social capital, with the school and its community becoming mutual providers of resources, expertise, employment and learning experiences, each to the other.
- makes full use of all that we now know about how humans learn so as to develop profound learning.

- gives increasing responsibility and leadership to young people for the conduct of their lives and learning, supporting their broader development as resilient, creative individuals, active citizens and enterprising workers.

In so doing, such a school aims both to raise the standards achieved by its students in traditional terms beyond the present plateaus, but at the same time also to measure itself by a broader range of outcomes. It is able to regenerate itself because it is looking outward to the regeneration of its communities, in which its students live and move, and to new relationships between school and the real world, the mainland and the island.

And as we shall soon discover, there are strong roots in both the past and present to support such thinking for the future, as well as the practical experience of a growing number of schools now acting as change agents.

Change Study 1
Kunskapsskolan, Sweden

www.kunskapsskolan.se

John Baumber

John Baumber is currently Director of Kunskapsskolan's Science Centre, Saltsjöbaden, Stockholm. He also leads, in England, quality assurance for the SSAT/ Quality Improvement Agency (QIA) training programme for Phase 1 of the 14–19 Diploma Support Programme. He speaks regularly at conferences, and carries out consultancy work on community leadership, personalization, international dimension, leadership and change management.

John has had extensive experience of school leadership, with four successful headships, most recently as Executive Principal of the Brook Learning Partnership in Bolton, England (2003–07).

His experience also includes establishing Bolton West Sixth Form federation, linking schools and training providers to provide holistic options for all post-16 learners. This involved setting up the Powerwave Skill Centres for Construction, Hospitality, Engineering and Land Based Study. John's vision for high-quality, collaborative provision to enhance learning opportunities for young people has involved him in developing schools as a central community resource, as well as leading a successful single regeneration bid to provide extensive community facilities and support operations.

IMAGINE being able to create a school that allows total flexibility over what is learned and how and when it is taught . . .

That is what Kunskapsskolan in Sweden have done over the last 7 years – not just once but 29 times to date. In fact, they have built a whole company of schools. They are part of a growing free school movement in Sweden, which now accounts for 15 per cent of Sweden's high school provision. But what distinguishes Kunskapsskolan from other schools in the sector is its clear learning structure and mission.

The diversity brought to the Swedish system by Kunskapsskolan can be best illustrated by a quick pen portrait of a school day. No bell marks its start. Learners arrive and go either into a learning environment or into the cafeteria, open space area. They are free to get down to work as they want. At 8.30 a.m. they go to their base room, with their tutor, in groups of about 20. Together they watch the News and spend some time discussing the issues. This is followed by a review of their log book and their short- and long-term targets. They draw up their plan for the day. Armed with a calendar of seminars they can attend, they review various stages and make their decisions about the programme. 'I'll not go to that maths session, because I am very confident that I understand and can complete this', might be a typical decision by the learner. They then choose the sort of space they need to go in order to work. They might prefer a quiet space on their own, or a group space to complete a teamwork aspect. Alternatively, they may decide to work in the cafeteria area and have a more relaxed learning period. Or they may decide they need to go to each seminar offered.

What happens is that each learner is in charge and owns their learning. They can decide to accelerate one aspect of the curriculum; they may decide to complete the outcomes in a range of unique ways rather than a prescribed route. Teachers stop being the purveyors of knowledge, and quickly become mentors and facilitators. They are free to extend the learning of their base or subject group to match their interests and abilities.

There is one important bit missing from this explanation however. The whole curriculum is managed by a sophisticated web portal, accessible from home or at school. The resources and process of learning are composed by the company's 700 teachers supported by headquarters' IT and pedagogical team. In fact, the central team manages most non-teaching needs – such as marketing, HR, repairs and maintenance – for the schools, working closely with the school leaders. Imagine the different working expectations of staff, and the freedom from endless preparation.

Kunskapsskolan, as a company, is 75 per cent owned by Kreab, 22 per cent is owned by INVESTOR, the largest investment company in the Nordic Region, and a small 6 per cent is owned by managers in the company. Over the first 4 years the company had to invest significant money from its own resources to enable it to grow, but now the company is profitable and its future secure. When the first five Kunskapsskolan schools were opened in 2000, the company would freely admit that they did not get everything about the school environment right. But as a learning organization, their later schools have created the sorts of spaces that match their unique curriculum plan.

Anders Hultin has been the driving force behind the Kunskapsskolan development, although he has now turned his attention to moving the concept outside Sweden, and Per Ledin, whose background is marketing, now heads up the organization of the company. The school teams are led by four key coordinators, two with responsibility for the 20 schools, one has responsibility for the growing sector of post-16 colleges, but the fourth has a cross-company responsibility for the company's pedagogy. This is crucial. There is an expectation that each school will follow the pedagogical principles and so achieve the aims of personalized learning for their young people. There are four key aspects to these principles.

Goal-orientated learning

Every learner knows the curriculum and expectations of each stage of the 4 years at Kunskapsskolan. As such they can plan their long-term goals. Many schools do this, but here the transparency of the task and curriculum enables them to break it down to semesters, weeks and days. Their log book is key to this, and each morning, like many people in work, they draw up their schedule. They know when seminars are taking place throughout the week and they can plan their time around these. As such they could be working with young people from different age groups.

Part of this process also includes finding the learning style that best suits your needs, enabling you to develop learning strategies to meet or exceed your goals. It may be a question of finding out where you learn best, or which study techniques will better help you to understand. Although they can follow a recommended structure they can also develop an individual way to meet their aims and achieve through a range of different means. Demonstrating achievement of a step does not mean the same outcome for every learner.

Personal supervision

Because teachers are not tied to lessons and are fully committed each day to taking groups of learners for particular topics, they are free to provide individual support and guidance. They will meet students in private, for at least a quarter of an hour each week, to make sure that work is progressing according to plan, that learners are finding their learning strategies, and to see whether they can challenge their limits a little more. As students learn to set goals and plan their time themselves, they will be allowed to take a greater responsibility for their own studies. The personal supervision is the most important factor in ensuring that the personalized education is really functioning properly.

The knowledge portal

The Knowledge Portal (Kunskapsporten) is the company's own internet web portal through which learners always have access to the school's educational aids and resources. They can reach it wherever there is an internet connection, from home and other places as well as from the school. Here are all the steps and courses, with proposed work procedures, tasks and resources in the form of texts, reference books, manuals, study tips, current news, etc. For each course, there are clear goals and descriptions of what you are expected to learn – and also what is required to achieve the Pass, Credit and Distinction grades.

Students, teachers and parents can follow how studies are progressing by reviewing the logbook, via the Pupil Documentation System and at the Knowledge Portal. There are some unique features that guide the curriculum. The four core subjects – Maths, Swedish, English and another Modern Language – are arranged in 35 steps, grouped in blocks of five. At the end of each block the student has to demonstrate they have mastered that aspect by passing a test, and completing a project, some of which is in the form of a group exercise. Students know that to pass they have to master step 20, and for a distinction step 35. Again they have choices to make, not just about speed of achievement but balance of effort between subjects.

Other subjects, including Science, are integrated into broad theme courses. So in Year 6, for instance, one course is 'Big Bang to Evolution'. This brings in both social and natural sciences. So whereas in an English school this might in the past have meant a study in geography of volcanoes and the earth's crust, while at a totally different time some of these are repeated and added to in Science as they study the cosmos and astronomy, here they form part of a coordinated programme with lots of opportunity for the development of themes to match particular interests. Art and Music and Technology also form part of this theme.

The route taken by each student depends on the challenge they create. They are shown three routes, with the 'black piste', as in skiing, being the most demanding and likely to enable them to achieve the highest of grades.

Rooms for learning

None of this can take place in conventional school architecture. So key to the development of each school has been the development of learning spaces to match the learning pedagogy. From the start of the company they have drawn on the skill and vision of architect Kenneth Gardestan to match the curriculum design.

Since everybody learns in different ways, the school's premises have been designed to meet the requirements of different pupils. They are modern and open, with space, glass and bright colours. Common features in most schools are the following:

The editorial office: a large open room, where pupils and teachers work together and the person who needs help always has somebody to ask.

The lecture hall: an amphitheatre for presentations, lectures or other gatherings.

Study rooms: of different sizes are available for individual studies, for conversations in couples or small groups, or for a class with about 20 pupils.

The café: which functions as a natural meeting place for pupils and teachers with space for both work and relaxation.

It would be wrong to paint this as a picture that has managed to achieve the ultimate in personalized learning. What, you may ask, of the less motivated learner? How do they cope? The schools have worked hard to ensure that, where learners significantly fail to achieve their short-term targets, greater intervention and support are brought in. However, the company is committed to each school becoming a 'pluggskolan', with all learners not just owning their learning but totally focused by their studies. They are taking a range of new measures to further enhance learning by adding greater challenge to their portal and supporting school leaders and teachers to develop and enrich all studies. This involves teachers working together with specialist teachers in subjects, developing specialist profiles and programmes for learners to choose.

To be able to match all aspects of a school to personalized learning is a rare opportunity. To do this as a company, with teachers working together to create a knowledge reservoir for learning, is very different from the experience of most school leaders and teachers.

The outcome is that, in the 28 municipalities in which Kunskapsskolan operates, most are in the top three schools. And at least one parent, Inger Svendsen, is delighted with this part of Sweden's school choice system. Her 14-year-old daughter, Paula, was unhappy at her local state school in Stockholm. A bright and independent-minded girl, Paula felt stifled by its formal teaching style.

Fortunately for Inger, under Sweden's school choice arrangements she was able to choose any other state school or a private school at no cost to herself. Sweden has a voucher system and as such it is possible for a range of individuals, companies and charities to open up their schools with Government and Municipal support. It means that each school, regardless of foundation, receives the same state funding. Sweden has a very strict policy that schooling should be free to all, and as a result very few parents choose to enter private education with a fee structure. It also has brought increasing diversity to the state provision.

As a result, Paula Svendsen now goes to the Kista Kunskapsskolan. According to Inger, it is very important for parents to make choices. Now she has changed to a very different type of school, Inger says Paula is 'much happier and studies better'.

Section 2
Understand . . .

The move from visions of the imagination to hard reality requires leadership and it takes planning, building and nurturing over time. These are themes that are taken up in later parts of this book. But before it can happen effectively, the initiation of change requires depth of understanding. An ability to move forward grows out of an understanding of how the present came to be, and what, from that experience, the levers for change might look like.

8   A brief history of school[15]

An understanding of the present begins with a view about the possible evolution of the concept of schooling itself. One way to understand the development of the school as an institution in society, and in particular its relationship with community, is to see it as moving through a number of broad phases. This does not mean these are steady, uniform, linear or clear cut. Rather there is a foggy, skeletal pattern, which may only be just faintly discernible, but one nevertheless on which it may be profitable to reflect. Such reflection can help us see more clearly how we might move forward from where we are towards the regenerating schools needed for the future.

Phase one – the statutory school

The first historical phase, beginning in England with the Education Act of 1870 and perhaps barely over now, saw the school simply as fulfilling a set of prescribed statutory functions in relation to the education of children and young people. Through these, it was believed, society and the child would gain. The extent of those functions and expectations has changed a bit over time, with successive Acts of Parliament, and not all of the functions may be universally agreed. They include prescribing to greater or lesser degree what should be taught, at what age it is taught, where it is taught and so on.

Some schools have always chosen themselves to exceed these expectations of their role. But what fundamentally governs this phase is the requirement of law, reflecting a wider expectation of society, governed particularly by the need to have an appropriate workforce for the needs of the industrial age. We could perhaps view this phase as like a simple diagram, where the circle represents the school (Figure 1).

Statutory
schooling

Figure 1 Phase 1

Phase two – dual use of the school, particularly its physical resource, for wider purposes

A second phase is now increasingly clearly acknowledged both in current UK government policy and educational practice, although it was common in many school settings over a good number of years in the last century. This phase sees the physical resource of the school as an economic and social resource for the wider community. Its facilities and resources can cost effectively be used for other purposes when not required for the school's main statutory duty. This extension of provision is commonly not led and managed from within the school. The term 'dual use' perhaps typifies the approach. Most recently in England, the extended school concept, where it is understood simply as co-location of services, perhaps exemplifies the thinking behind this phase at its highest level.

In this view, the school site provides an institutional base. The functions may (or may not) connect, but, if they do, it is only at the periphery. They do not impact in any way directly on the education of young people. They are often separately managed, and plan their development in isolation. They may communicate, and sometimes collaborate on specifics, but the purposes of each remain firmly their own (see Figure 2).

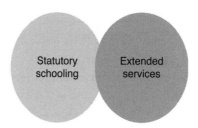

Statutory schooling

Extended services

Figure 2 Phase 2 - The school begins to be seen as a wider resource

Phase three – sharing a wider ambition

But for some schools already, the use of its facilities by other parties, whether or not in the context of extended schooling, is but part of a wider ambition, which might be described as to build social capital.

Social capital is a term that has grown into the jargon of community development over the last decade and it is a useful shorthand for us. Robert Putnam, one of the key thinkers behind it, defines social capital as:

features of social life – networks, norms, and trust – that enable participants to act together more effectively to pursue shared objectives.[16]

Whereas physical capital refers to physical objects, and human capital refers to the properties of individuals, social capital refers to connections among individuals – social networks and the norms of reciprocity and trustworthiness that arise from them. It is about a network of reciprocal social relations. A society of many virtuous but isolated individuals is not necessarily rich in social capital.

The argument is then that high-trust societies have an enormous competitive advantage over legalistic societies, in which suspicion of people is a cultural value. This is because the transaction costs go down in high-trust organizations. For example, if people in two different departments or regions (say, marketing and sales, or Asia and Europe) feel enough trust to speak candidly together about their impressions of the market, the quality of work processes and ways to improve the work, then they have many more opportunities to innovate and think together. The cost of new projects goes down accordingly. Whether high trust applies to a country or a company, the outcome is the same: more value is created when expensive, unwieldy oversight is reduced.

In the case of schooling, this means educational achievement is likely to rise significantly, and the quality of day-to-day interaction is likely to be enhanced, by a much greater emphasis on fostering trust and confidence from those around them in order to thrive. Effective schools are to a significant degree about shared objectives with parents and with others. It is worth taking time and trouble to secure this trust because it can result in real benefits for both the community and the school. And research evidence is now beginning to suggest that social capital can be a key influence on long-term school achievement.[17]

Investment in building social capital is thus not about pure altruism on the part of a school, it is an integral part of core business. That is the core of this argument about the significance of social capital for schools.

But, for many schools operating in this phase currently, the building of social capital is simply seen as a bridge, an important but subsidiary purpose. The school's activities in this area do not necessarily impact very directly on what students experience in the classroom. The school does not have a direct responsibility for learning within its wider community. However, it does nevertheless act as an important repository of trust, and is a key locus for a range of networks. It does seek to involve parents in particular, but perhaps others as well, in providing some moral and practical support for its statutory roles.

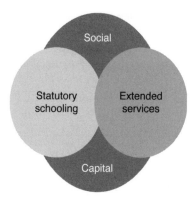

Figure 3 Phase 3 - The shifting emphasis in the purpose of schools – from educational achievement to building social capital

A further development within this phase has been the beginning of the understanding that schools, important though they might be, cannot do everything. Not every service or every learning activity needs to be located in the school. Indeed there is a real place for learning in the community. In terms of extended schools, the shift of language now towards extended services is in part a reflection of this.

The insight that learning can take place beyond school, but that there needs to be a real and dynamic interaction with school, begins to mark a move away from a purely provision-led model of schooling, in both its statutory and extended forms, towards an awareness of the need for a depth and breadth of community engagement, one of the prime defining characteristics of a fourth phase of development – the phase of regeneration.

In diagrammatic terms, the shifting emphasis in this third phase of development could perhaps be represented as in Figure 3.

Phase four? – the regenerating school

The village college would change the whole face of the problem of rural education. As the community centre of the neighbourhood it would provide for the whole man, and abolish the duality of education and ordinary life. It would not only be the training ground for the art of living, but the place in which life is lived, the environment of a genuine corporate life. The dismal dispute of vocational and non-vocational education would not arise in it. It would be a visible demonstration in stone of the continuity and never-ceasingness of education. There would be no 'leaving school'! – the child would enter at three and leave the college only in extreme old age. It would have the virtue of being local so that it would enhance the quality of actual life as it is lived from day to day – the supreme object of education.. . . It would not be divorced from the normal environment of those who would frequent it from day to day, or from that great educational institution, the family . . .. The village college could lie athwart the daily lives of the community it served; and in it the conditions would be realised under which education would not be an escape from reality, but an enrichment and transformation of it. For education is committed to the view that the ideal order and the actual order can ultimately be made one.[18]

Those words were penned by Henry Morris in 1926 to describe what, as Chief Education Officer for Cambridgeshire County Council, he wanted to create as new schools in Cambridgeshire, in response to what was known at the time as 'the rural problem', the relative poverty of the countryside compared with towns, and the consequent population drift, which left behind remote, scattered and impoverished communities. His words now feel rather dated in some of the language. But they do, nonetheless, describe a different, vibrant and largely still unrealized, view of the school's role as a social capital builder. This vision sees the school as a core social centre. A prime purpose of the school here is to build social capital through learning, as an integral and overarching part of both its statutory and broader purposes.

It is, in turn, possible, even likely, that this development would impact in changing the nature of those extended services being provided through the school's agency, as they in turn draw on the enhanced social capital created. Meanwhile the nature of the school itself is transformed, as it becomes an integral part of the mainland, and no longer an island.

To a significant extent, our task in discovering and understanding the regenerating school may be to re-imagine the concept of the village college of the early part of the last century for the very different world of today and, more especially, tomorrow. In diagrammatic form, this new direction might be represented as in Figure 4.

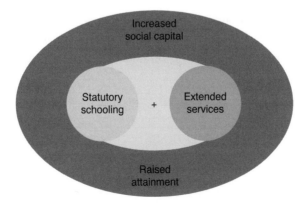

Figure 4 Phase 4 - Discovering and understanding the regenerating school

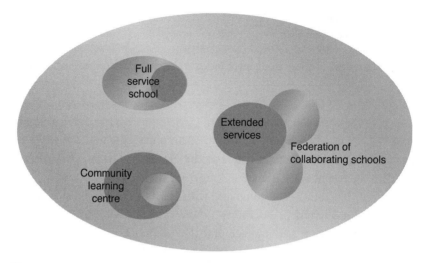

Figure 5 Three examples of a mature approach to integrating learning and extended services

But what this diagram doesn't show at all clearly is that a concept of regeneration may also significantly be about groups of schools not just individual schools in isolation. For no one school serves a community alone. It is part of a network of schools across ages, types and geography. There is a shared collective moral responsibility for the well-being of all young people within localities, which is in turn a share of all schools' responsibilities towards all the nation's young people.

At the risk of the diagrams becoming too complicated, a final picture might illustrate this further extension of the fourth phase – with some of the possible models of a multi-site educational provision as schools look beyond individual units to forms of collaboration and federation.

Figure 5 shows just three examples of a mature approach to providing learning – a federation of schools jointly accessing extended services, a full service school providing a wide range of extended services and a community learning centre that as part of its provision offers education and training.

9 From village college to community college – the Sawtry experience[19]

In England, the Cambridgeshire experience, through over 80 years of grappling with understanding and implementing the concept behind the village college ideal, highlights both some of the potential and the difficulties inherent in turning imagination into reality.

The gestation and development of the original village colleges were not easy. They were marked by significant funding issues, political battles and personality clashes. Progress was often slow. The first college opened at Sawston in 1928 and was quickly surrounded by controversies, as Harry Ree described in his book *Educator Extraordinary*.[20] Other colleges followed, with not inconsiderable struggle because of the difficulties in funding them as something 'different'. The quality of architecture, of fitting out, and of environment, were all crucially important to Morris, who had a very clear view that the village college was not a school, let alone a school with extra bits tacked on. He regularly visited 'his' colleges, and on one occasion complained bitterly to the Warden, the term he chose in preference to headteacher to signify the wider community leadership role that was envisaged, 'You're making this place look like a school'.[21]

By the 1970s, the county of Cambridgeshire had expanded geographically to include the areas of Huntingdon, Peterborough and the Fens. Each component local authority had begun to build schools with community facilities. But a Phase 2-type dual-use interpretation often prevailed. For instance, in new community colleges built to support the development of new townships, co-location of sports facilities was common, but with distinct management, usually by the district council who had the funding responsibility for sport, as opposed to the county council who had the funding responsibility for schools.

Many involved felt there was a stagnation of the idea and a general lack of new progress at this time, but the advent of a new 'hung' council early in the 1980s, breaking from a long tradition of Conservative administration, led to a major review and a restatement of policy.

In 1984, Cambridgeshire County Council published 'The Community's Education'. This ambitious policy statement envisaged every school having some sort of community engagement, within coordinated planning and provision across a small local area. In a real sense, it could be argued, this thinking was ahead of its time in understanding the need for coordination of services and provision to meet the needs and wishes of learners. However, before the policy could take real effect, power and possibility passed away as a result of political changes at the local and national levels, and the funding to help make it at all achievable progressively disappeared.

The 1988 Education Act resulted among other things in the disaggregation of individual budgets for schools and the very important beginning of school-based financial management. But combined with an ongoing bearing down by central government on levels of public spending, and with 'non-statutory' areas bearing the brunt, this began a steady year-by-year contraction of community education activity, in Cambridgeshire and elsewhere, with, inevitably, a resulting loss of focus and momentum.

At this point, real pioneers look to sidestep the constraints and move outside the box of current orthodoxy. One such example is in Sawtry, just off the main A1 road between Huntingdon and Peterborough. Through clarity of purpose and flexibility of approach, the evolution of Sawtry's village college illustrates how it was possible to retain and develop community engagement to raise standards and improve services against such a backdrop of financial restraint and limitation by thinking through new structures and approaches to resourcing and partnership.

In 1992, Sawtry Village College became a grant-maintained school, under the then government policy, partly in order to secure provision for sixth-form education in the local area and also to begin to redesign its approach to community engagement. To mark this change of approach, the College decided to move away from its traditional Village College title to a new name, which included the word community. Sawtry Community College was born.

In order to maintain and develop community education, facilities and services, a new company, called Multitask, was then formed. This was a registered company limited by guarantee (that is, not for profit). A Managing Director, Alan Stevens, was appointed who also became an Associate Principal of the College. The company was made accountable to the Governing Body through a community subcommittee.

Over the next 15 years a range of other transformations followed, characterized by the application of innovative and flexible thinking. For instance, the college had traditionally offered a crèche to people while they attended an adult education course or leisure activity on site. This was very costly and gradually became unable to meet new regulations for childcare. In 1994, Dawn Quince drew up a plan to locate a privately run day nursery on the College site. The College provided an appropriate piece of land, and Dawn provided new portable buildings that met all the relevant regulations. The college offered a lease arrangement on the land and charges an annual rent. College staff, students and the local community now benefit from excellent crèche and day nursery facilities.

Working at the opposite end of the age spectrum, Marjorie Dybeck had founded CARESCO around 30 years earlier to offer care and resources to senior citizens in the community. It was unique to Sawtry. In the 1990s, the organization was located during the day in the adult common room within the school building and in an old mobile classroom outside. However, facilities were becoming poor, funding low, and the College was expanding and needing more space. But, rather than removing this facility, the College identified a piece of unused land and offered this on a long-term lease. This enabled the CARESCO team to bid to the national Lottery for funds to build a new purpose-built care centre. This CARESCO Centre receives a grant from the local authority but also fundraises as a registered charity to expand the range of support it offers.

Having both a Day Nursery and Care Centre on site of course offers unique opportunities for college students to participate in a range of purposeful volunteering and vocational work experience. Strong links have been developed with the College's curriculum-based Citizenship and Social Enterprise schemes.

In another example of lateral thinking, Huntingdonshire District Council in 1994 took out a 30-year lease on the College Sports Centre and funded the building of a new community swimming pool. They took on the responsibility to staff and manage a community Leisure Centre, with local primary schools and the College buying in, on an annual basis, swimming and sports hall time in the school term. The College governors and senior staff sit on the joint management committee with representatives from the District and County Councils. Partnership working then enabled a joint bid to go to Sport England to fund an extension to the Leisure Centre, which included fitness suite, dance studio, new changing rooms, crèche and public foyer area. The successful application would not have been possible without the joint working between different Councils and community partners. The new Leisure Centre serves a larger population throughout the year and offers a higher standard of service and excellent facilities than the College alone could economically have offered.

And in order for the village of Sawtry, with a population of 7,000 people, to have a Public Library, the local authority now pay an annual rent for sharing the College's Learning Resource Centre. This arrangement enables a Public Library to exist in the village and gives the general public to access a wide range of resources and free internet access. The College's library staff and the public library staff work closely together, offering a better and more cost-effective service than either could provide alone. By working together in this way, new schemes and funding are also attracted to the area. Thus, in 1998, the College became a school partner with Microsoft UK to pilot Anytime Anywhere Learning.

This scheme enabled students at the College and adults in the community to access learning via the internet and laptop computers. Community tutors piloted IT courses in village halls by taking a dozen laptops out in their car and linking up to the internet via telephone lines or wireless connectivity. A regional IT test centre was established next to the Public Library. This was able to offer online tests for Royal Society for the Encouragement of Arts, Manufacture and Commerce (RSA), Computer Literacy and Information Technology (CLAIT), European Computer Driving License (ECDL) and Microsoft courses, with a fully qualified assessor present. The IT Resource Centre provided a high-quality IT facility for both the school and community. It offered IT courses and video conferencing facilities to local business groups, which in turn brought in additional income to ensure staff and facilities costs are covered.

As a result, the College is able to offer excellent facilities to local businesses and to host conferences, creating revenue through hiring out the Conference Room, while the College catering service also benefits from servicing conference events. By upgrading facilities and having a business-critical approach, the college has been able to play an important role in lifelong learning in the business sector, culminating in 2004, when it became a government-funded Training School, providing the opportunity for professional development, as well as ICT competency programmes, coordinated and delivered through Multitask.

In all these ways, over a period of years, through the school working together with this wide range of partners, the village of Sawtry has gained excellent facilities in a rural area, which could not be sustained by any one organization alone. It is the creative collaboration of several organizations that pulls together a community to ensure that everyone can benefit from using shared facilities on a learning campus, which is in turn part of a connected learning community. And the opportunities available to school students are hugely enriched at the same time.

Regeneration at Sawtry Community College has relied upon leaders being pioneering in creating organizational structures and collaborative partnerships with the private and public sector organizations. There has been clarity of purpose to secure and further develop opportunities for all its citizens to access world-class courses, facilities and services, in support of a culture of lifelong learning.

10 A mirror image for specialist schools

One key strategy in Sawtry's development turned out to be the early use of specialist Technology College status, with its additional government funding, to help pursue its wider ends. This originally quite exclusive and divisive initiative by the Conservative government of the day evolved into a genuine attempt to change schools for a different future, and contained sufficient incentive and opportunity to help start a profound process of change in many of the country's schools. It has become perhaps the major driving force of change in English secondary education for the last decade, and is a key locus in government policy for much of its current aspiration for school and community engagement.

To some extent our four suggested phases mirror the evolution of this Specialist Schools Initiative in its understanding of community engagement. The programme began in the early 1990s clearly rooted in Phase 1 thinking. Schools passed through a competitive and reasonably demanding bidding process. In return for additional funds they would meet challenging targets. The performance change sought for the individual school was defined exclusively in narrow 'statutory' terms, crudely speaking improved GCSE results.

But in 1997, a major policy shift from the incoming Labour government began to embrace a broader notion. It recognized very clearly that differential funding for the few could not be justified. Equally there was not enough immediately available in the public purse to make those sums available to all. Moreover even if there were, it might not deliver benefit in terms of improved outcomes if it did not carry a real incentive to change and to do some things differently. This dilemma was resolved in the realization by government that continuation of funding for those already receiving it needed to be matched to an expectation they shared their resources and expertise with others, while, progressively, similar additional resources and responsibilities were made available to all who could demonstrate credible plans for improvement. From this insight grew the community element of the specialist schools programme, a requirement for schools receiving this extra funding to share more widely the resources and the expertise they developed as a result.

Initially, this community dimension was conceived simply as sharing with a family of schools, that is local primary schools, which most secondary schools found quite easy to do, as there is a strong element of self-interest involved here. The extension to other secondary schools, though, they often found more problematic in an environment of strong competition among schools.

But soon after its introduction, this element grew to take on a notion of the wider community and the school's contribution to that, albeit in somewhat prescribed ways and quite possibly with a fairly narrow understanding of the interaction between school and community. Gradually, though, over a number of years, this understanding has opened out. The most recent (2007) guidance for specialist schools produced by the Department for Children, Schools and Families (DCSF) says that:

> The community element . . . (is) . . . an integral part of the (specialist school) plan and reflects a school's engagement with, and through, its community.[22]

Phases 2 and 3 in our model mirror this growing awareness and broadening understanding within the specialist school initiative, through its increasing emphasis on forms of collaboration and mutually beneficial partnership. It is some of those specialist schools, their partnerships and federations, that now, as they grapple with the possibility of fourth-phase development, strain at the leash to point the way to possible transformation into schools that are centres of regeneration. The Brook Learning Partnership featured in Change Study 2 provides just one example.

11 Change in a world of change

Schools seeking such transformation do not, though, seek it in a stable context. It seems inevitable that schools over the next 10–15 years will eventually see significant change in the way they are structured and in their relationship to society. But the concept of the regenerating school is by no means the only possible outcome from this period of ferment. The case needs to be put, more forcibly and more widely than it often has been, to win that argument.

A useful guide to the alternatives that might arise was first published by the OECD in 2001.[23] This document pictures six scenarios for the future of schooling by the year 2020. These scenarios grow out of a detailed analysis of a number of trend factors.

The changing nature of childhood and extending adolescence

The idyllic view of children playing with friends in the street, or reading a book at the end of school has disappeared from many Western societies. It has been calculated that children in the UK aged 11–15 years now spend 53 hours a week watching TV and computers, an increase of 40 per cent in a decade. About half of children now have a TV set in their bedrooms. Eighty-seven per cent have a mobile phone or their own web page or blog. Without doubt this has had significant positive and negative impacts. It has been linked with negative impacts such as obesity, violent behaviour, back pain/bad posture, short-sightedness and early puberty. Positively it has been said to aid speech development, help with understanding and education, raise awareness of important issues and current affairs, and to help forge social bonds.

Its impact on education and learning is potentially massive both in terms of the demand for a type of delivery matching the rapid fire computer game or high resolution of TV, and in the opportunity for varied approaches and locations for learning. It has in many ways removed some of the innocence of childhood and the cohesiveness of family life, not least, because the young now inhabit a different world. A recent report 'Their Space', from the think tank Demos, examines carefully the discontinuity between this world and the world of adults and decision-makers and explores some of its implications for schools.[24] The Demos report sets out a clear challenge to adults and to schools:

> The current generation of decision-makers – from politicians to teachers – see the world from a very different perspective to the generation of young people who do not remember life without instant answers from the internet or instant communications from mobile phones. It is these decision makers who shape the way that digital technologies are used in the system and who set them up to limit their use and role in everyday life. This is a short term solution to a long term change.

The phenomenon of precocious puberty – when children develop the first signs of puberty earlier than the normal ages of 10 years for girls and 11½ years for boys – is increasing all over the Western World. In 1990, the first signs of precocious puberty were around the age of 8 years for girls, the whole process taking 2 years to complete. Now, according to Professor Salti from the University of Florence,[25] some children enter puberty as young as 7 years. Boys, too, are entering puberty at an earlier stage, albeit still slightly later than girls.

Conversely, the increased school-leaving age, which in many Western European countries, as it will soon formally be in England, is basically 18 years, delays the time when young people become independent and wage earning. This extended education is widely held to be a good thing, but it does put different stresses on both family budgets and life, and brings a need for more diverse education and training to match the greater social maturity of young people. Particularly in an increasingly materialistic West, the pressure on young people to have their own income and independence means many young people are running dual lives of study and earning, with all the concomitant pressures that brings.

The growth of the global knowledge economy

As far back as 1970, Alvin Toffler recognized the pressure of ever-increasing change will have, and subtitled his book *Future Shock* with the warning:

> The symptoms of future shock are with us now. This book will help us survive the collision with tomorrow.[26]

Simply expressed, the story of the book is 'too much change in too short a time'. Such level of change or rather the discontinuity between one level of development and the next has been defined by the word 'revolution' – the agricultural revolution, the industrial revolution. Tom Stonier in his book *The Wealth of Information* clearly recognized we are at a new information revolution point. Not only is this a technology step-change, it is the access to information that is the real wealth creator and power broker.

> Political power is shifting from the owners of capital to the professional bureaucrats and technocrats – the purveyors of information.[27]

But not everyone today is by any means a 'knowledge worker'. Many continue to occupy low-skill positions, but with increasing job insecurity, especially among the less qualified. So the OECD report sums this challenge up perfectly when it 'wonders' about the capacity of many school systems to address such a broad and challenging knowledge agenda, one that goes well beyond traditional conceptions of educational quality and the 'know-what' focus of factual knowledge/recall. Much of what was taught within the school curriculum is in any case forgotten by adulthood. This, combined with the quickening change in job-related knowledge requirements and the greater complexity and diversity of the pathways through adult life, poses searching questions about how education equips students for the future. Paradoxically, perhaps, the very importance of knowledge in the twenty-first century may increase, not diminish, the need for schools to place a strong emphasis on establishing a healthy personal and social foundation in the young, in order to give them the tools with which to cope with the complex, rapidly changing world in which they live. Many of those tools are about personal development and citizenship rather than cognitive knowledge.

This has been exemplified clearly in the recent Leitch Report[28] into the state of skills in the UK, and by the redesign of the whole curriculum including the introduction of new 14–19 Diplomas. Leitch argues that Britain, and coincidentally much of Western Europe, has to recognize that it will need to operate in the higher skill areas on the global stage, and present measures will only maintain a shrunken share of the job market. It is the wider range of personal and thinking skills that will be important to produce teamworkers, active researchers and reflective thinkers. In other words, future workers have to have the skills to manage this hurricane of expanding and changing information, and discriminate as to what needs to be used, extended and developed.

The impact of social exclusion

The last century saw enormous progress in raising standards of living and the quality of life for many people. However, in almost every country around the world the gap between the richest and poorest members of communities has been widening, particularly in the last 30 years. Although older members of populations, and those established in work, have done relatively well, younger members of the population (including children) and those with precarious labour market positions have done badly.

Take the US. Since the early 1990s economic progress has been robust and steady. At least until 2007, inflation was near zero and unemployment at implausibly low levels. However despite that, the poorest and least educated have experienced a fall in standards of living for the last 25 years. The wealthiest 20 per cent of households in 1973 accounted for 44 per cent of the income. By 2002 this had risen to 50 per cent, while everyone else's fell. The bottom fifth saw their meagre 4.2 per cent slip to 3.5 per cent in the same period. Interestingly, in 2007 China reported almost similar discrepancies in incomes.

At a local or regional level the impact can be even starker. Although the number of children nationally living in poverty in the UK is 21 per cent, some city areas record figures between 60 and 70 per cent.

Much of this discrepancy is related to the very changes outlined previously, with an ever-decreasing need for low skills. But in a society where increasingly access to information and technology is essential, this group risks becoming ever more excluded from society.

The changing nature of family and community life

The decline of the neighbourhood community and the traditional family has radically altered the support structures in which young people grow up. Declining birth rates and greater material wealth have helped shape different values and preferences in society. In many Western societies, this has been augmented by the declining influences of religious and secular groups. Increased marital dissolution, teenage pregnancy, and a greater mobility and transience, all impact on the well-being of children and the security they may experience in society. The decline of the conventional nuclear family can often mean close family support in times of family stress is not consistently available.

Many young people are perfectly able to cope and in fact know no other life than this one. But, for others, choices and decisions that they make impact greatly on their lives. The US still has the highest teenage pregnancy rates matched against comparable economies, although now declining. Three in ten girls become pregnant before they are 20 years – that is 750,000 teen pregnancies annually. Early pregnancy and childbearing are closely linked to a host of other critical social issues, including poverty and income disparity, overall child well-being and education to name but a few. Teen childbearing costs the US taxpayer US$9 billion each year.

In this new, more open society, some have identified the school as a key part of a mission to reorder and organize support at a neighbourhood level. In the UK, the development of extended schools is a direct response to this. The OECD report suggests schools and the wider community need to ask if this socialization role needs to be more explicitly stated and developed.

> This would be to recognize the potential of the school as the communal setting critical for the upbringing of the young, where contacts, friendships, play and informal learning are essential rather than incidental. While this should not necessarily conflict with a strong focus on student cognitive development, it requires investment in a very broad set of educational outcomes, going well beyond the measurable aspects of student achievement if this mission is to be brought about.

Inequalities between rich and poor countries and much more

The trends discussed so far have referred primarily to the situation in OECD countries. What of the rest of the world? First, the inequalities between the rich and poor countries of the world have been widening at an alarming rate:

> Inequalities continued to grow over the 20th century, though also comparatively slowly until well into the post Second World War period. From 1960 onwards they soared: from 30 to 1 in 1960, to 60 to 1 in 1990 and 74 to 1 at present. Inequality is still increasing, in countries and between countries.

This is indeed very rapid change, and should inform thinking about the communities in which students will live as citizens now and in the future. But more recently, we have begun to recognize that the global economy is an even more complicated picture and the relationship among countries is complex and inter-related. Thomas Friedman begins his book *The World is Flat: A Brief History of the 21st Century*:

> No one ever gave me directions like this on a golf course before: 'Aim for Microsoft or IBM'. I was standing on the first tee at the KGA Golf Club in downtown Bangalore, in southern India . . . .. The Goldman Sachs Building wasn't done yet . . . HP and Texas Instruments had their offices by the back nine.[29]

This clearly illustrates the phenomenal change in parts of India as the West outsources work there, but it also recognizes the real potential of skilled workers elsewhere in the world. It is much more complicated than taking low-wage, low-prestige jobs from America and finding in India they are high-wage, high-prestige jobs with a more motivated workforce. New technologies are allowing Indians to start taking higher paid system-design jobs that had previously been the exclusive domain of Americans, for instance.

And then there is China, soon to become the largest English-speaking country in the world, and the Middle East, shaped by the power of oil money with all the ensuing political complications. This is a much more complicated world than Rich World, Poor World, or First World, Third World. However we define it, our young people need to be prepared for this complexity and ensure they understand the impact of the global economy on their future prospects and their own priorities for education and training.

Population growth and diversity

It is expected that by 2025, the relative share of population within OECD countries will have fallen from 19 per cent in 1999 to 16 per cent. Nevertheless, the pressures pushing people from poor countries to rich countries will continue to be intense, while the birth rate in those more well-off countries is likely to remain relatively low. The impact is then to see greater cultural and ethnic diversity. Net immigration generated two-thirds of the increase in the UK's population between 2001 and 2004, and more recently the country has seen significant immigration from within the enlarged European Community. Inevitably this brings a new pressure to schools in terms of supporting integration and specifically providing support with English. However, the bigger challenge is how well schools are able to provide a social anchor for all their learners, and equip them with the skills and values to live and work in such a rich and diverse environment.

Pulling together the implications of all these six factors and thinking about how schooling might respond requires a clear, strategic approach. The regenerating school thinks not just about what it needs to do over the next year to continue its improvements, but takes a wide view of these future issues. It is looking at the wider context of the next 10–15 years and how the school might respond to external change. This shapes its core strategic intent and allows a more flexible and long-term direction to emerge. It also protects the school from the short-term vicissitudes of national and local policy.

Over the last two decades, we have seen significant reductions in autocracy at all levels. The arrangement whereby decisions can be made centrally and imposed on others only has a short-term life. At a family level, many of the changes discussed above have led to young people exercising greater choice over their own environment and future. At a national level, we have seen devolution of powers to regional governments and the break-up of countries into smaller more autonomous units. The nature of our knowledge society, with its rapid communications and exposure to a wide range of cultures, allows small states not just to survive but to excel, and allows individuals to exercise their rights over access to information.

So at a school level, the regenerating school needs to empower its learners and its teachers to 'design and build' their school collaboratively and to personalize learning. Centrally controlled schools, managed from afar, will not only fail to meet the challenge, they will fail to prepare their learners with the skills to live in this new and changing world.

12 De-school, re-school – or what?

The six snapshots that follow attempt to convey the essence of each of the six scenarios developed by OECD to show possibilities inherent in responding to this environment and the change factors that are shaping it. The scenarios are not intended to be necessarily mutually exclusive. Elements of each could come together in different permutations. Some do clearly lend themselves much more towards the possible development of the regenerating school and some appear to move in quite different directions.

The scenarios are classified into three broad groups, each with a further subdivision. The classifications are about maintaining the status quo, re-schooling or de-schooling. Let us consider each in a bit more detail, drawing on the very clear and helpful summary published by the National College for School Leadership.[30]

Group 1-Maintaining the status quo

A. Bureaucratic school systems continue

This scenario is built on the continuation of powerful bureaucratic systems, strong pressures towards uniformity and resistance to radical change. Schools are highly distinct institutions, knitted together within complex administrative arrangements. Political and media commentaries are frequently critical in tone; despite the criticisms, radical change is resisted. Many fear that alternatives would not address fundamental tasks such as guardianship and socialization, alongside the goals relating to cognitive knowledge and diplomas, nor deliver equality of opportunity. Under this scenario, we might see the following features:

Learning and organization: Curriculum and qualifications are centralized areas of policy, and student assessments are key elements of accountability, even though questions persist over how far these develop capacities to learn. Individual classroom and teacher models remain dominant.

Management and governance: Priority is given to administration and capacity to handle accountability pressures, with strong emphasis on efficiency. The nation (or state/province in federal systems) remains central, but faces tensions due to, for example, decentralization, corporate interests in learning markets and globalization.

Resources and infrastructure: There is no major increase in overall funding, while the continual extension of schools' remits with new social responsibilities further stretches resources. The use of ICT continues to grow without changing schools' main organizational structures.

Teachers: A distinct cadre of teachers exists as a professional group, sometimes with civil service status; unions and professional associations are strong but professional status and rewards problematic.

B. Teacher exodus – the meltdown scenario

This scenario envisages a major crisis of teacher shortages, highly resistant to conventional policy responses. It is triggered by a rapidly ageing profession, exacerbated by low teacher morale and buoyant opportunities in more attractive graduate jobs. The large size of the teaching force makes improvements in relative attractiveness costly, with long lead times for measures to show tangible results on overall numbers. There would be disparities in the depth of the crisis by socio-geographic, as well as subject, area. Very different outcomes could follow: at one extreme, a vicious circle of retrenchment and conflict; at the other, emergency strategies spur radical in novation and collective change. In this scenario, we might see the following features:

Learning and organization: Where teacher shortages are acute they have detrimental effects on student learning. We find widely different organizational responses to shortages – some traditional, some highly innovative – and possibly greater use of ICT.

Management and governance: Crisis management predominates. Even in areas spared the worst difficulties, a fortress mentality prevails. National authorities are initially strengthened, acquiring extended powers in the face of crisis. A competitive international teaching market develops apace.

Resources and infrastructure: As the crisis takes hold, funds flow increasingly into salaries to attract more teachers, with possible detrimental consequences for investments in areas such as ICT and physical infrastructure. Whether these imbalances would be rectified depend on the strategies adopted to escape 'meltdown'.

Teachers: The crisis, in part caused by teaching's unattractiveness, would worsen with growing shortages, especially in the most affected areas. General teacher rewards and the distinctiveness of the cadre of teachers could well increase due to the relative scarcity of staff. Established arrangements may eventually erode with 'meltdown'.

Group 2-Re-schooling

C. Schools as core social centres

The school in this scenario enjoys widespread recognition as the most effective bulwark against social, family and community fragmentation. It is now heavily defined by collective and community tasks. This leads to extensive shared responsibilities between schools and other community bodies, sources of expertise and institutions of further and continuing education, shaping, not conflicting with, high teacher professionalism. Generous levels of financial support are needed to meet demanding requirements for quality learning environments in all communities and to ensure elevated esteem for teachers and schools. Under this scenario, we might see the following features:

Learning and organization: The focus of learning broadens with more explicit attention given to non-cognitive outcomes, values and citizenship. A wide range of organizational forms and settings emerge, with strong emphasis on non-formal learning.

Management and governance: Management is complex as the school is in dynamic interplay with diverse community interests and of formal and non-formal programmes. Leadership is widely distributed and often collective. Local decision-making is strong, while drawing on well-developed national/international support frameworks, particularly where social infrastructure is the weakest.

Resources and infrastructure: Significant investments would be made to update the quality of premises and equipment in general, to open school facilities to the community, and to ensure that the divides of affluence and social capital do not widen. ICT is used extensively, especially its communication capabilities.

Teachers: There is a core of high-status teaching professionals, with varied contractual arrangements and conditions, though with good rewards for all. Around this core would be many other professionals, community players, parents, etc., and a blurring of roles.

D. Schools as focused learning organizations

Schools here are revitalized around a strong knowledge agenda rather than a social agenda, in a culture of high-quality experimentation, diversity and innovation. New forms of evaluation and competence assessment flourish. ICT is used extensively alongside other learning media, traditional and new. Knowledge management moves to the fore, and the very large majority of schools justify the label 'learning organizations' (so equality of opportunity is the norm), with extensive links to tertiary education and other organizations. Under this scenario, we might see the following features:

Learning and organization: Demanding expectations for teaching and learning combine with widespread development of specialisms and diversity of organizational forms. Flourishing research on pedagogy and the science of learning is systematically applied.

Management and governance: 'Learning organization' schools are characterized by flat hierarchy structures, using teams, networks and diverse sources of expertise. Quality norms typically replace regulatory and punitive accountability approaches. Decision-making is rooted within schools and the profession, with the close involvement of parents, organizations and tertiary education, and with well-developed guiding frameworks and support systems.

Resources and infrastructure: Substantial investments are made in all aspects of schooling, especially in disadvantaged communities, to develop flexible, state-of-the-art facilities. Extensive use is made of ICT. The partnerships with organizations and tertiary education enhance the diversity of educational plant and facilities.

Teachers: They are highly motivated enjoying favourable conditions, with strong emphasis on research and development, continuous professional development, group activities and networking (including internationally). Contractual arrangements might well be diverse, with mobility in and out of teaching.

Group 3-De-schooling

E. Learning networks and the network society

Dissatisfaction with institutionalized provision and diversified demand leads to the abandonment of schools in favour of a multitude of learning networks, quickened by the extensive possibilities of powerful, inexpensive ICT. The de-institutionalization, even dismantling, of school systems is part of the emerging 'network society'. Various cultural, religious and community voices come to the fore in the socialization and learning arrangements for children, some very local in character, others using distance and cross-border networking. Under this scenario, we might see the following features:

Learning and organization: Greater expression is given to learning for different cultures and values through networks of community interests. Small group, home schooling and individualized arrangements become widespread.

Management and governance: With schooling assured through interlocking networks, authority becomes widely diffused. There is a substantial reduction of existing patterns of governance and accountability, though public policy responsibilities might still include addressing the 'digital divide', some regulation and framework-setting and overseeing remaining schools.

Resources and infrastructure: There would be a substantial reduction in public facilities and institutionalized premises. Whether there would be an overall reduction in learning resources is hard to predict, though major investments in ICT could be expected. Diseconomies of small scale, with schooling organized by groups and individuals, might limit new investments.

Teachers: There is no longer reliance on particular professionals called 'teachers': the demarcations between teacher and student, parent and teacher, education and community, break down. New learning professionals emerge, whether employed locally to teach or act as consultants.

F. Extending the market model

Existing market features in education are significantly extended as governments encourage diversification in a broader environment of market-led change. This is fuelled by dissatisfaction by 'strategic consumers' in cultures where schooling is commonly viewed as a private as well as a public good. Many new providers are stimulated to come into the learning market, encouraged by reforms of funding structures, incentives and regulation. Flourishing indicators, measures and accreditation arrangements start to displace direct public monitoring and curriculum regulation. Innovation abounds, as do painful transitions and inequalities. Under this scenario, we might see the following features:

Learning and organization: The most valued learning is importantly determined by choices and demands – whether of those buying educational services or of those, such as employers, giving market value to different forms of learning routes. A strong focus on non-cognitive outcomes and values might be expected to emerge. There is wide organizational diversity.

Management and governance: There is a substantially reduced role for public education authorities. They oversee market regulation but have less involvement in organizing provision or steering and monitoring. Entrepreneurial management modes are more prominent. Information and guidance services and indicators and competence assessments that provide market currency play important roles.

Resources and infrastructure: Funding arrangements and incentives are critical in shaping learning markets and determining absolute levels of resources. A wide range of market-driven changes would be introduced into the ownership and running of the learning infrastructure, some highly innovative and with the extensive use of ICT. Problems might be the diseconomies of scale and the inequalities associated with market failure.

Teachers: New learning professionals – public, private, full-time, part-time – are created in the learning markets, and new training and accreditation opportunities would emerge for them. Market forces might see these professionals in much readier supply in areas of residential desirability and/or learning market opportunity than elsewhere.

Dean Fink, writing about the challenges facing leaders of schools, describes the multi-faceted environment that shapes our schools. He likens this to 'Jake the Peg', the song made popular by Rolf Harris, in which a three-legged man struggles to know which leg to put forward first.[31] He believes that school leaders in the twenty-first century have one leg still working in hierarchical bureaucracies, one leg in a new public management with its state curricula, standardized tests and site-based management, while having a third leg in learning networks as they try to refocus their school onto students' learning. We explore later the leadership skills required to operate in this context, but here it illustrates the need to not look at these scenarios as singularities. Reality and solution perhaps draw on a number of elements of each scenario.

What does this mean for the concept of the regenerating school? Well, there are many successful schools that can be seen as part of bureaucratic and administrative systems as in the first scenario. In many ways, parents and the wider community have a very con-servative view of schooling. Moving away from this presents risk. If we see schools as delivering just a quantifiable outcome of traditional results, then 'good' schools will look for every way they can to enable learners to achieve that standard, regardless of whether or not that equips young people for the future and gives them the skills to meet a new twenty-first-century world.

But it is clear that, whatever we may think we know this next decade will bring in terms of a future world, it is likely we will fall short in our imagination. In a challenging paper, Futurelab[32] seeks to explain the real difficulty of trying to predict the future.

> We only have to look back to the 1970s to witness the prediction that only three computers would be required worldwide, for example; or to the 60s to witness the predictions that we would be

shortly be living on the moon in fetching silver jump suits. The pace of technological change is both more rapid than we can ever predict and monumentally slower than we ever thought possible. This is not only because it is sometimes harder to achieve the breakthrough we had intended or indeed easier because developments in one field unexpectedly assist research in another (think of the implication for human genomics of the massive increase in computer processing power over the last ten years). It is also because technologies enter into already existing social spaces – they are shaped by existing social practices, human interactions and values they encounter outside the laboratory. Again we only have to look to the history of the record player. This device was originally intended as a personal recording machine rather than a replay tool which would spawn an entire industry and transform musical practices around the world.

The paper goes on to predict some radical changes that technological developments may already be bringing to everyday learning and working life. It raises fundamental questions for educators. For example, if we are able to progress faster and further what we learn, understand or achieve through the use of technologies, such as microcomputers and telephony, should we, when we assess young people, be assessing what they know or what they can do with these tools and devices? After all, which will they need to do in work and life?

It would be easy to be paralysed by the anxiety of what the future might bring and how education might respond. But, as Douglas Adams once wrote, 'The best way to predict the future is to build it'. And that is exactly what regenerating schools do! They make sure that they know what they would like to achieve and then they use the technology available at that time to achieve it. It is not the technology that is the objective, rather it is the means to that end.

So, turning back to the six scenarios, the rapidly changing environment in which we live can actively encourage us to look at re-schooling ideas as a basis for a future vision for schooling, while recognizing that, if we can use technology to study anything any-where at any rate, the concept of a school itself might be outdated in its present forms. Some schools have already been very enterprising in the development of online learning so that students ostensibly become remote learners for another institution. It might even be that some aspects of learning could be delivered by something that is not a school at all but a commercial operation. A regenerating school sees learning as being wider than just its own pupils but about its whole community. It seeks to bring the breadth of that com-munity experience into its resource portfolio and so will exploit all these avenues and opportunities. After all, if the future employee has to be flexible, adaptable, creative and an independent lifelong learner, then schooling should in some way resemble that world.

The regenerating school is sharply aware of the pedagogical expertise it can bring to help learners discriminate the best way to learn and the best type of support they will need so as to achieve. But that pedagogy and practice need to reflect the way of the world now experienced by young people. It needs to recognize the immense opportunities young people have for communicating their ideas with others and testing their opinions, and the power available to them for informal learning. England is currently investing billions of pounds rebuilding its schools, and has invested unprecedented amounts in information technology in schools. These investments alone do not recognize the new digital environment. They do not automatically represent re-schooling. That remains a key role for leaders of regenerating schools – to create the best future they can.

13   Getting personal

The six scenarios, and the underlying trend factors they represent, form part of the established backdrop to the possibility of creating more regenerating schools that are in turn helping to regenerate those around them. But those trends are also informing wider debate about the future of public services in the UK, all of which are subject to the same forces for change as schools. Any serious thinking about the future of school and community will therefore need to recognize and take a view on the risks and opportunities to which the wider reform of public services might give rise, while at the same time looking to address these proactively so as to secure a preferred outcome. At the heart of the public sector reform agenda lies current debates around personalization and choice, contestability and accountability, in the development of public services.

Charles Leadbeater, one of the leading exponents of a changed approach to public services, pictures personalization in a school context like this.[33] He describes schools as 'solutions assemblers', helping children and young people gain access to the mix and range of learning resources they need. He suggests it is only possible to assemble solutions personalized to individual need if services work in partnership. Schools should therefore be gateways to networks of public provision, while sharing resources and becoming centres of excellence.

As a result, he comments,

> If personalisation re-writes the role of the user, it is inevitable that the role of the producers will also have to shift. Innovation comes through producers and users working together to develop solutions. Imagining the implications of this in relation to education suggests some far-reaching changes to the workforce and the kinds of skills that professionals will need.
>
> As part of the solutions that the school offers, it might engage with other providers, such as social services, to meet the need of the 'whole child', the needs of every aspect of each of their learners. This engagement with a broader community implies significant shifts – *not only in the culture but also the practical aspects of a school*.

The emphasis in the last sentence is mine. Here is further reinforcement to the idea that pursuit of the standards agenda alone is no longer enough, and that the broader outcomes we need require a different concept of school. However, effective implementation of this policy direction also leads to further questions. What might such a school actually look like? How might we go about building one, in terms of its culture as much as its physical presence?

At the same time there is here a further key insight as to why a new approach to community engagement is needed by schools. As well as contributing to the long-term raising of attainment through their impact on building social capital, regenerating schools, even though they may not necessarily be schools as we currently know them, have a significant contribution to make to the policy aspirations for 'Every Child Matters'.

Through 'Every Child Matters', the UK Government's aim is for every child, whatever their background or their circumstances, to have the support they need to achieve five outcomes. All children will:

- be healthy
- stay safe
- enjoy and achieve
- make a positive contribution
- achieve economic well-being

A Government Green Paper, published in 2003, alongside the formal response to the report into the death of Victoria Climbié, a young girl who was horrifically abused, tortured and eventually killed by her great aunt and the man with whom they lived, built on existing plans to strengthen preventative services by focusing on four key themes:

- Increasing the focus on supporting families and carers – the most critical influence on children's lives.
- Ensuring necessary intervention takes place before children reach crisis point and protecting children from falling through the net.
- Addressing the underlying problems of weak accountability and poor integration identified in the Climbié report.
- Ensuring that the people working with children are valued, rewarded and trained.

That Green Paper prompted an unprecedented debate about services for children, young people and families. Following the consultation, the Government published 'Every Child Matters: the Next Steps', and passed the Children Act 2004, providing the legislative spine for developing more effective and accessible services focused around the needs of children, young people and families. As a result, a major realignment of both local and national governments has taken place, with Directors and Departments of Education being replaced by Directors and Departments of Children's Services at a local level, opening up new configurations of education, social services and health provision.

Mohammed Mehmet was one of the first Directors of Children's Services to be appointed into this new role. He came to the unitary authority of Peterborough to begin to bring together education services and social services for children and young people into a coherent whole, with integrated working with health a longer term goal as well.

The hardest challenges he found began with what he terms 'respective professional ignorance and preciousness about roles'. Established services competed for resources and hence for power and influence. As a result, it was clear to him children were falling through the gap between schools and social services, and this could not change without attitudes changing. The key issues confronting the new service, therefore, were about changing approaches to leadership and about getting everyone to think things through together from the perspective of the child or young person. Taken together they represent a major and continuing challenge in change management.

The national culmination of these developments, in policy terms, occurred in 2007, when the then-new Prime Minister, Gordon Brown, abolished the former Department for Education and Skills, and replaced it with two new departments, the Department for Children, Schools and Families (DCSF) and the Department for Innovation, Universities and Skills (DIUS). That change within its first months gave rise to some significant new emphases from DCSF in particular.

Within a remarkably short space of time, 6 months later, the new department published the 'Children's Plan' setting out the range of its aspirations for families, children and young people through to the year 2020, with detailed targets and also significant links suggested between school and community.

> We want to build on the ambitions set out in 'Every Child Matters', and deliver a step change in outcomes. We will:
>
> - expect every school to be uncompromising in its ambitions for achievement, *sitting at the heart of the community it serves*
> - set high expectations for Children's Trusts to:
>   o deliver measurable improvements for all children and young people
>   o have in place by 2010 consistent, high quality arrangements to provide identification and early intervention for all children and young people who need additional help
>   o enhance children and young people's wellbeing, particularly at key transition points in their lives.[34]

In the UK, this ambition has been the culmination of a long journey, with earlier steps, such as the launch of the Children's Fund in 2000, paving the way for the cultural change that is still needed in the way support services to children and young people are organized. Under that programme, Local Authorities were required to establish partnerships of services and providers that would address the gap in preventative services for children and young people at risk of exclusion by increasing and better coordinating preventative services. In other words, it is about seeking to target children and families at risk rather than waiting for problems to emerge. That means working closely with parents and young people who are hard to reach by traditional services, and listening and responding to their needs.

Sometimes voluntary groups can be far better at reaching this audience. They are free of the stigma some people feel about being involved with social services. They can be more flexible in their approach. Such voluntary groups vary enormously in scale and size. Some are large national organizations with multi-million-pound budgets, while others are simply collections of local people who have come together to provide sustained facilities for young people or families. It is crucial to recognize the potential partnerships that schools and statutory bodies can have with both such groups in order to get the best coordinated mix of services.

ARK (Absolute Return for Kids), for example, provides grants to charities and charitable projects. It is an international charity that treats its grants as investments to maximize social return. It applies business principles and standards, wherever appropriate, and sees itself as a swing investor to each project, often acting as a bridge funder until government is ready to follow the example created. One example is its work with Fairbridge, a charity working in 15 of the most disadvantaged urban areas in the UK and supporting 13–25 year olds who are no longer in education or training and excluded from many aspects of society.

Claire is typical of a beneficiary of this programme.[35] She had been taking part in a Fairbridge programme for 7 months. Claire is a 15 year old, confident, likeable young lady with a cheery disposition, but when she first joined Fairbridge her temper often got the better of her.

> I was really angry with everything. If someone made even the slightest comment I would just snap. I used to take offence.

Her quick temper made it hard for Claire to progress in school and she struggled academically. When her teacher suggested working with Fairbridge she was a little apprehensive.

> I didn't really know what to expect, all I knew was that I needed to calm down. I thought I'd give it a try because I wanted to do better in school and aim higher, I just didn't know how to.

With Fairbridge, Claire took part in activities such as hiking, abseiling, rock scrambling and orienteering as well as garage and metal workshops.

I've learnt so much. Fairbridge is better than just being sat round all the time. Now I know what there is out there for you when you are older, and I know there is more out there for me.

As Claire completed the different activities, her confidence grew. She learnt to remove herself from situations when she can feel her temper rising, and her teachers commented that she is much calmer. Her relationship with her father also improved: 'He trusts me now and I'm always truthful with him'. Claire developed interpersonal skills with other people 'I'm more social with everyone, not just people I know'. A school report commented that:

Claire has been able to transfer the skills learnt at Fairbridge back to school. She is happy to put her hand at anything, comfortable in taking a lead role and good at encouraging others to get involved.

Helped by her support worker, Claire looks to the future. She would like to work with older people, as well as get six GCSE qualifications to 'make her Nanna proud'. Learning to cope with herself and other people has been a major step forward for Claire, who thinks that without Fairbridge she wouldn't be the person she is today.

If Fairbridge can help me they can help anyone! Although I'm nervous about going for job interviews and stuff, Fairbridge has given me the confidence to get back on track with my life.

So, the development of integrated services for children provides a new context for schools, and opportunity for a wider view of the support that young people may need. It is not only statutory bodies that can provide such services. There is ample evidence of the strength to be gained through working with voluntary groups and also empowering neighbourhood communities to take ownership of programmes.

Internationally, the picture is very varied and the approach equally diverse. Compare, for instance, the UK approach with the major educational initiative in the US 'No Child Left Behind'. In 2002, President Bush signed this landmark act, which imposed targets on state authorities to raise the scores of young people in standardized tests so that by 2014 every child is achieving the grade level. The US government would cite success as follows:

- More reading progress has been made by 9 year olds in 5 years than in the previous 28 years.
- Maths scores for fourth and eighth graders have reached new heights.
- Achievement gaps between African-American 9 year olds and their white peers have fallen to all-time lows.
- Significant investment has been made into teacher training and the testing of young people.

However, there is also significant criticism about this narrow approach to improving standards. In literacy, for instance, 2006 showed that fourth graders had slipped from fourth in the world to eleventh behind Russia, Hungary and Singapore. A teacher from Noralto School in Sacramento, California, described the policy as 'tearing her school apart'.[36] Her students come from underprivileged families, mostly arriving with little or no English, relying on the school as a pillar in their lives. Many parents are unable to provide the academic support the students need, and nearly all the students struggle with language barriers. Consequently most are below the grade level. Schools failing to reach this level for 2 years are classed for Programme Improvement. In the Programme for 5 years, the Act allows for the school to have new staff appointed to 'wipe the slate clean', despite seeing improvements year on year. The teacher, writing in the *San Francisco Chronicle*, claims the programme is sucking the joy out of the school.

> A teacher's job is to breathe life into education and to get children to love learning. Creating rigorous testing is simply creating an oppressive system in which music, physical education and social studies are fading into non-existence. At my school, a specialist has created a bell-to-bell schedule, in which every minute of the day is mapped out. We are told what and how to teach, what to put on the walls and what interventions to provide. All assemblies and field trips are banned.

Whatever the truth about the success or flaws of the policy, this story illustrates the real dilemmas and challenges facing schools and governments across the Western World. We must be able to compete on the world economic stage. Yet at the same time we must also fundamentally change our view of what economic success looks like in order to secure a sustainable future for the planet, and we must turn around the ever-increasing gap between richest and poorest sectors. We must achieve higher standards if we are to succeed. Yet successful learning and the wider raising of attainment also require curiosity and passion. The one cannot be at the expense of the other. And the challenges involved in creating a sustainable future require wholly new skills, thinking and leadership.

To state all that is also to make a statement of moral purpose and moral responsibility, and the challenge is to achieve that purpose for all. The nature of the schools and the structures around them that we create will be key to that success. To make that happen, it is time to get serious about Phase 4 thinking. And we do stand at a moment of particular opportunity and challenge in the UK. A combination of political shift, growing awareness and education policy direction could combine to give real and rapid impetus to regeneration. That outcome is not, though, a given. Success will need imagination and clarity as to where we are heading and why, along with commitment to press ahead with the journey.

Change Study 2
The Brook Learning Partnership, Bolton, England

www.thebrooklearningpartnership.co.uk

John Baumber

Imagine a school which realizes that, for the long term, the benefits of collaboration far outweigh the short-term gains of competition . . .

So it is with the Brook Learning Partnership, itself a partnership of two schools in Bolton, England. Rivington and Blackrod High School, the larger school with some 1,900 students, has a history going back over 450 years. As such it has long held an important place in the heart of the community, although it is now much transformed from its original small grammar school tradition. Its heavy oversubscription was in marked contrast to another school, situated towards the centre of town which could only attract 70 learners, and which was closed in 2004 having failed to improve over 3 years from being in special measures. And so The Brook Learning Partnership was formed as that school, now called Ladybridge High, was reopened as a part of a hard federation with Rivington and Blackrod, with one Executive Head and one Governing Body.

In a way, this development epitomizes the mission of Rivington and Blackrod. Two years earlier the school had established two important long-term partnerships. The Horwich and Blackrod Learning Community, a partnership with nine local primary schools led to childcare in the primary sector and a wide range of out-of-school activity based in three hub primary schools. Bolton West, a partnership to provide joined-up post-16 provision between two High Schools, the local FE College and Alliance Learning, a work-based learning provider, leads in key new curriculum initiatives such as the introduction of the UK's new 14–19 Diplomas and the provision of a wide range of vocational courses – construction, land-based studies, engineering, catering, and hair and beauty. The schools have common timetables and jointly appointed specialist staff focusing on raising achievement.

The federation with Ladybridge High School has had significant impact not just on the educational outputs in both schools but on the very structure and capacity of the two organizations. Crucially it was part of Rivington's strategic purpose to follow this route. The school's track record of establishing partnerships recognizes three levels:

1. Organizations coming together for a specific project.
2. Organizations networking together to share good practice and learn together.
3. Organizations that have a shared destiny and see their work in the longer and medium term delivering larger collaborative gain than individually they might achieve.

The head, John Baumber, brought this approach in 1998 from his first headship in Northumberland. There, all high schools have community status and responsibility for local adult education and youth provision. Working with partners in the community – churches, Town and District councils, the schools, voluntary groups and local industry – the school set about championing a community-wide approach to learning, which led to enhanced youth provision, networked working across the schools, health care drop-ins and information points, a full-time drop-in facility for adult learners, and new leisure and recreation facilities. It was essentially about building a confidence in the town of Prudhoe that people had the capacity to move forward and make a difference, not just for young people but also for the whole area.

Rivington and Blackrod High School did not have that formal 'community' status and worked in a more centralized environment, although the community had similar issues. Because it is located on the edge of Bolton, the community often felt that things were done to it rather than taking active control to influence and develop. Out of this, the Horwich and Blackrod Learning Community was formed in 1999 by the nine primary schools in the two towns and Rivington and Blackrod High School. Together they identified objectives, and set about making it happen. Very soon they achieved three successes – specialist technology status for the High School, a Lottery award for the development of summer schools, after-school clubs and childcare, and a European project to develop IT learning across the community.

Each could have been seen as individual and short-term projects, but because the partnership had identified a core purpose and mission, they instead formed the springboard for a wide range of community learning activities. Each partner took responsibility for leading some aspect of the work. This was crucial to maintaining ownership and extending capacity.

From this initial success, the partners agreed to the appointment of a coordinator to network, manage the project and seek continued sustainable funding. Michelle Howard's appointment, with her marketing and business background, became fundamental to the partnership. Meeting partners, being part of wider groups charged with community development, and then managing the finance and workforce issues, let alone individual funding requirements, is more than a full-time job.

The school then tried to address its objective to increase post-16 participation rates. The school had a small and very successful sixth form, but the focus on academic A levels meant that significant numbers of students did not see this as a route for them. The school realized this was something which limited aspiration and opportunity. It also meant many young people were travelling outside the community for post-16 education.

Again, rather than developing an aggressive marketing strategy for its wider curriculum plan, it looked to other providers locally and created Bolton West. This collaboration, comprising two high schools with sixth forms, the local further education college and a work-based-learning provider, developed a wider curriculum offer and a joint prospectus, which meant learners had the opportunity to study a comprehensive range of levels and subjects, both academic and vocational. Again the partnership took the decision to appoint a full-time coordinator, and Geraldine Rafferty, like Michelle, helped make a reality of the strategic decisions taken by the group. Both coordinators generate so much new business that they more than pay back their salary to the partnership.

The success here has led to the expansion of the partnership to include all 11–16 schools in the area and extended the focus to 14–19 provision. The schools now have a joint timetable 2 days a week for learners aged 14–16 years that has enabled a wide range of vocational provision. The partnership, under their POWERWAVE brand name, has championed provision for Level 1 learners and now provides programmes in Catering, Land-Based Studies and Construction. In fact with the latter two, they now provide for schools across Bolton with over 300 learners taking advantage of facilities and expertise. The schools also have joint staffing in the form of Science and English Advocates, whose specific role is to work with the Heads of Department to strengthen performance and opportunity in these areas. What is more the partnership has the maturity to be happy about resources being deployed according to need rather than a rigorous equal share to all each year. They are interested in joint outcomes.

One can easily sense how the development of the Brook Learning Partnership, with its wider links, could quickly bring benefits and capacity to the new Ladybridge High School. The two schools worked together to ensure that Ladybridge quickly attained specialist Sports College status. All Heads of Departments worked together to share curriculum resources and design. Pastoral leaders worked closely together to support learners in a multi-agency environment. However, within just 3 years the improvements at Ladybridge meant that they not only were recipients of support but could also share their expertise and experience across the partnership.

Each school is very different and serves different communities. As such it is important that they have the opportunity to develop their own response to local situations. This brings real richness to the partnership, as does the fact that restarting a school allows for a radical review of structures. So for instance, Ladybridge has a 4½-day-teaching week with Tuesday afternoons given over to extracurricular activity and staff training. Rivington and Blackrod are planning to move to this model as soon as possible. The school also has a radical approach to special needs with transition classes in Year 7 having a more primary-age focus to curriculum delivery. Again Rivington has drawn on this experience. In return, the development of the diploma in Land-Based Study at Ladybridge will draw clearly on the POWERWAVE brand and Rivington's Construction centre.

But, as in Northumberland, Brook's strategic purpose is not just about a relevant curriculum with effective teaching and learning. It is about understanding the nature of learners and their wider social context. Without doing this, significant numbers of young people would continue to be excluded from the success of others. As a result of this approach to working with all Children's Services partners, the schools have been really successful in the development of extended services. They have attracted two cohorts of Lottery funding to establish youth provision and adolescent health work. Originally youth work took place with small numbers of boys in a rundown centre with just 12 hours a week of youth time. There was no work with younger children despite the real need in part of the schools more deprived catchment area. Working with a neighbouring primary school, they developed a shared administration entrance, with in-school youth facilities for 9–12 year olds. The new Centre was refurbished and renamed and the staffing quadrupled. Staff were appointed jointly, so that there was another arm to the schools' pastoral support programme. Sometimes a youth worker is able to support young people and counsel them better than teachers, and the changed environment can make the start of a real difference in their approach to learning and self.

But most recently, the Brook Learning Partnership has been committed to developing a more extended, multi-agency approach. The schools do not believe they can provide quality educational opportunities for all their learners if they fail to recognize their social and development needs. They have established a local Pupil Referral Unit, managed directly by the schools' pastoral teams, coordinated youth provision in the town, and most recently have established an adolescent health project with health and youth services. Out of this engagement with health services, the schools are now working on a project focused on improving health by providing sensitive health information and support.

The community is responding to the national and local authority agenda, but personalizing resources to meet their own circumstances. Key to this is the voice of the young people and other stakeholders. The schools have used a range of techniques to both fashion and oversee this work, including focus groups and a technique for community engagement known as Future Search, which is described in Section 3 (Plan . . .).

Above all they have recognized that there are two key requirements to operate in the way described here. First, you have to invest in your own staff and ensure a level of commitment to this broader vision of education. Rivington has become a Training School and is one of just eight 'Investors in People Champions' in the UK.

Secondly, you need a capacity and skill in networking and in understanding the local, regional and national environments. The Brook Partnership has made it a priority to appoint key staff without teaching background or roles in order to drive this agenda forward.

Section 3
Plan . . .

The regenerating and regenerated school which we need for the future, with roots in the past as well as in some current directions of UK government policy, is in fact about becoming a school which consciously and coherently:

- connects schooling directly to real-world experience, including the involvement of a wide range of people sharing their knowledge, ideas and skills, and acting as co-educators.
- contributes to increased social capital, with the school and its community becoming mutual providers of resources, expertise, employment and learning experiences, each to the other.
- makes full use of all that we now know about how humans learn so as to develop profound learning.
- gives increasing responsibility and leadership to young people for the conduct of their lives and learning, supporting their broader development as resilient, creative individuals, active citizens and enterprising workers.

In so doing, it aims both to raise standards achieved by its students beyond present plateaus and also to measure achievement by a broader range of outcomes, and in particular those that impact on their ability to live and work in a future none of us can imagine. Such a school is able to achieve that regeneration of itself, its work and its purpose, precisely because it looks outward to the regeneration of its communities. And it is through its engagement with its communities that it also becomes able to regenerate itself.

14   Five threads of change

These are not new ideas, as we have seen, but they do have a particular resonance today in the different, globalized, flat world we now inhabit. There is also urgency in understanding and applying them if the opportunity of the moment in England in terms of policy refocusing at the centre of government through the pursuit of the 'Every Child Matters' agenda is not to be lost. Even the Audit Commission, which some might perhaps regard as the most unlikely body to think in these broader, possibly less quantifiable, terms, has not only got the message – they have also clearly understood it. In their report, referred to in Section 1 (Imagine . . .), they put it like this.[37]

> Schools need to develop a clear individual vision, incorporated within school plans, which sets out the school's role in the local area and how the school will work with the whole range of local public services in support of both school and community success. Schools need to promote an ethos among staff, pupils and parents where the school is seen as a community resource and there are high expectations for pupils and the community alike.

The report goes on to identify a number of key features of the changes that are needed. Schools, they argue, need to ensure

- partnership working with local public services, the community and other schools is integrated into the vision, management plans and day-to-day working of the school;
- support for families is seen as central to better educational outcomes;
- the concept of community goes wider than children and parents;
- the school is seen as a community resource by staff, pupils, governors and local people;
- the school is responsive to community concerns;
- there are high expectations and aspirations for pupils and the local community alike; and
- community engagement is promoted as important for all staff.

That summarizes extraordinarily well the increasingly recognized need for all schools today. Its force derives in part from a school's distinctive position as the social institution with a presence in every community. For every family has contact at some time with a school. A school is a huge physical resource, as well as, in many communities, one of the largest employers. But the force of the argument also derives from an understanding that schools cannot now succeed in those new terms that our unknown and unknowable future requires without responding to the need for real community engagement.

Every school has the capacity to be regenerating. It is not dependent on investment or buildings or resources. But that does not mean every school is actively working as a force for regeneration. Some still do inhabit the island, and remain disconnected from the mainland. The regenerating school, though, does not appear from nowhere, out of nothing. Change will not just happen without conscious intent, and clear, shared moral purpose.

No school, not even one which is newly established, begins with a completely clean sheet. It exists within a context particular to itself and with expectations held by others, which may or may not be conducive to change. The first need, therefore, is to understand that context through immersion and analysis. The capacity to take on the features and characteristics of regeneration grows through deliberate and conscious effort, building out from that which already exists with a clear long-term strategy. A school seeking to develop towards a fourth-phase identity, through growing its capacity for regeneration, needs to accurately assess its starting point. It needs to be able to articulate what needs to change, and why, and how that can come about. In short, it needs its own narrative to convey the nature and meaning of the journey it is seeking to make.

Such a narrative can be built around five threads of change, each of which provides a spectrum of development, against which a school can map where it is in relation to where it aspires to be. Taken together, those threads provide, through their interlinking and intertwining, a strong central core around which to grow and develop.

The five threads[38] are introduced here in outline and their underpinning basis is explored in this chapter. The first three threads are then examined in more detail in Section 4 (Build . . .), and the final two form the basis for Section 5 (Lead . . .).

Thread 1 – ethos and culture

Every school establishes its own ethos through its physical and its emotional environment. The regenerating school consciously sets out to create an open, humane and welcoming environment, a climate conducive to good relationships and good learning for all, and one which values equally its statutory and extended functions.

The regenerating school sees, and is moving towards, a close and inextricable linkage between its required and necessary purpose of statutory schooling and the learning needs of the whole community. That does not mean these are necessarily one and the same thing. 'Holistic' might be a word to describe the underlying thinking. The connections between the two are understood, used to inform planning and decision-making, and exploited for learning gain, wherever possible.

It is possible for a school to do this because it has given careful thought to the way in which it presents itself to others. 'Openness' might be a word to describe this trait. It would include the physical opening of buildings for many days of the year and for much of the day, but it is about much more than being simply a hirer of space. The regenerating school looks to create interaction and partnership. Openness, therefore, extends beyond the building to address the way in which people, and their ideas, are received or welcomed. The open building cannot succeed in its wider educational purpose without an open welcome and open manner.

The ethos of the regenerating school is developed in such a way that it recognizes the rights and fosters the responsibilities of staff, students, parents and all who are part of the school at any level. These approaches combine care for others, empathy, responsibility, environmental respect, the ability to make informed decisions and opportunities for effective participation. They require:

- continued development of qualities of openness in communication, decision-making and relationships
- a humane development of the physical environment
- strategies that promote the self-esteem of students, staff and others
- the creation and use of opportunities for celebration of citizenship and leadership

Thread 2 – promotion of learning

Every school identifies teaching and learning as its core business. The regenerating school consciously sets out to develop, among all those with whom it has a relationship and a responsibility, the capacity and motivation to learn for themselves to the highest levels of which they are capable, along with the flexibility and agility to continue this throughout their life.

In order to try to meet its larger conception of its role, the regenerating school creates flexibility within itself, and the capability to respond to opportunity as it arises. It tries to make sure, in particular, that the opportunities for its students' personal development that are made available through its wider role are fully utilized.

So within its curriculum, the regenerating school:

- understands the significance of its role in fostering the skills and attitudes of lifelong learning
- reflects to some extent local concerns and community in its curriculum
- seeks opportunities to move the locus of some learning beyond the school gates
- recognizes and fosters ways for the community to take on a role as co-educator
- recognizes and values the potential contribution young people can make to the learning and well-being of others.

Effective approaches to the promotion of lifelong learning place emphasis on individuals and their learning needs, prioritizing and targeting those individual needs well. They place emphasis on the autonomy of the learner, taking a flexible approach to capture the 'learning moment', and reviewing learning and acknowledging progress frequently.

But promotion of lifelong learning also has a wider community dimension. It, therefore, fosters the rights and responsibilities of learners, encourages active citizenship and fosters both independence and interdependence. It understands the importance of first-hand experience in developing these skills and attitudes.

Thread 3 – building social capital

Every school makes an impact on the present and future prospects of its various communities. The regenerating school realises its potential to contribute to confident and resourceful communities, particularly among those least advantaged, and actively plans and implements strategies to secure long-term renewal and sustainability.

Although definitions of community development are numerous and varied, the central premise within any understanding revolves around concepts of communally felt needs and self help. One writer has summed up its outcome as

voluntary activity by local residents to meet their collective need, overcome disadvantage and improve conditions and opportunities in that locality.[39]

Community development in the context of education is about learning, particularly that which helps learners both to take responsibility for their own learning and lives and to contribute actively and effectively to a wider community. Developing self-esteem and interpersonal skills through co-operation and collaboration is thus a key focus. And principles of equal opportunities also imply an imperative to seek for all equal access to the structures of power and decision-making.

Thread 4 – connectivity

Every school forms part of a wider network of care and responsibility. The regenerating school understands and proactively engages in strong, effective and reciprocal partnerships to support its core and wider purposes, in which it is at various times both leader and contributor.

The regenerating school is engaged in a two-way traffic and two-way dialogue with its community. It will move outside its walls, not just to meet and work with people where they are but also to involve the community in helping it fulfil both its statutory and its extended educational roles.

Too often a partnership is just a collection of people from different organizations who happen to be present in the same room, 'giving the impression of dancing together while actually standing still', as Drew Mackie vividly puts it.[40] But that does not give rise to regeneration.

Thread 5 – empowerment

Every school has processes through which it is governed, led and managed. The regenerating school takes active steps to ensure that its decision-making processes are open and transparent. It takes steps implicitly and explicitly to engage and empower all its stakeholders. It understands the importance and inevitability of conflict between groups and positively develops its capacity to manage and respond to such conflict creatively.

The regenerating school has an acute understanding of the loose–tight balance between its values and way it goes about things. It has the ability and commitment to look and go beyond its own campus, working with others on their terms and in their locations. It does not draw everything into the school itself or into its control. It will seek to afford power to communities and a measure of community control over its work, management and resources. It understands the importance of consciously identifying and analysing local learning. It actively engages with its partner local schools in a shared responsibility for all children and young people. And it develops mechanisms to reach out to those who might slip through the net or otherwise not come into contact, perhaps drawing in, for instance, the support of a voluntary or community organization or an outreach worker.

The regenerating school also fully understands that this is not a message about motherhood and apple pie. Conflict is a necessary and inevitable part of community, and the ability to handle the conflict that arises, and to turn it to non-destructive and productive ends, is a key but neglected role, in which a school can play a crucial educative role.

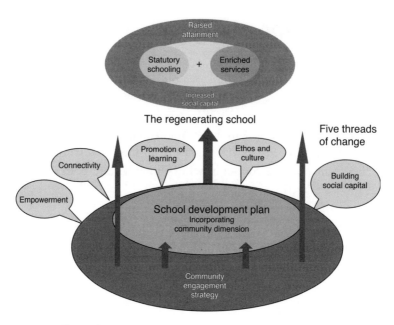

Figure 6 The reinforcing effect of the five threads of change

These five threads of change can combine to create a powerful linkage and synergy. And indeed a major element for any school, in building its own narrative around them, lies in the intentional and planned interweaving of all the threads to create a reinforcing effect. But what binds the elements together is an underlying focus on community engagement, re-creating the relationships between school and community.

This means any school looking to build its capacity for regeneration needs to ground its work in a considered strategy for community engagement. It also means its community role is centrally linked into its planning for whole school development. And, for specialist schools in England, this is exactly what is now expected of them in terms of their continuing designation and funding. That move has the real potential to begin to create the fourth phase school of our imaginings.

We can perhaps represent this underpinning role of community engagement, and its connection to school planning and the threads of change, visually through a further refinement of the diagrammatic models in Section 2 (Understand . . .) (see Figure 6).

15 Understanding community engagement

If that is a picture of aspiration for all schools, then a key starting point for the journey is to be clear what effective community engagement means and looks like. As a concept, community engagement has been around in policy and ideas circles beyond education for a number of years, but there is not really a common or widely agreed definition. The term has become part of the jargon of New Labour government in the UK, and various studies and reports provide various definitions. This one is taken from the Department for Communities and Local Government website in 2007, and serves as well as any. Community engagement is seen here as being about involving people in decisions that affect them. It is

> the process of working collaboratively with and through groups of people affiliated by geographic proximity, special interest, or similar situations to address issues affecting the well being of those people.

There are inevitably, of course, different levels of such engagement that might be possible. Sherry Arnstein, writing in 1969 about citizen involvement in planning processes in the US, described such levels in terms of a ladder of participation.[41] In her view it had eight rungs.

Rung 1 – Manipulation and Rung 2 – Therapy- are both non-participative. The aim here is to cure or educate the participants. The proposed plan is self-evidently the best. The job of participation is to achieve public support for it through some form of public relations exercise.

Rung 3 – Informing – is an important first step to legitimate participation. But too frequently the emphasis here, says Arnstein, is on a one-way flow of information with no channel for feedback.

Rung 4 – Consultation – may be a legitimate step. It might include, for instance, attitude surveys, neighbourhood meetings or public enquiries. But Arnstein argues this is still just a window dressing ritual that offers little real power in decision-making to the community.

The next step, Rung 5 – Placation- might cover, for example, the co-option of hand-picked 'worthies' onto committees. It allows citizens to advise or plan ad infinitum but retains for power holders the right to judge the legitimacy or feasibility of the advice.

Rung 6 – Partnership, begins to redistribute power through negotiation between citizens and the holders of power. Planning and decision-making responsibilities are shared, perhaps through joint committees.

Rung 7 – Delegated Power – sees citizens holding a clear majority of seats on committees with delegated powers to make decisions. The public now has the power to assure accountability of the programme to them.

On the final rung – Citizen Control – have-nots handle the entire job of planning, policy-making and managing a programme. An example here might be neighbourhood corporations with no intermediaries between it and the source of funds.

Arnstein's ladder of participation strongly suggests in the descriptors used that some levels are better than others. The higher up the ladder the more real the participation, and indeed the descriptions of lower rungs are quite dismissive of their place.

But it may be that a ladder is not the best image to choose, with its implication of a single pathway and upward travel. It may be that in reality there is not a straight upward progression and that various styles have a place according to both time and context. The different levels, whether described exactly in Arnstein's language or not, may each be appropriate at particular moments. It may be necessary to both climb and descend steps on this ladder, time and time again. Depending on the objectives, the issue and the community to be engaged with, some patterns of movement might be more suitable than others and may not actually follow straight lines of travel.

David Wilcox has developed a model, based on a simpler and perhaps more balanced ladder of participation, to define the stages of community engagement by which those in authority relate to citizens around common issues.[42] His model has five components, which he describes as follows:

- Informing – this is about giving a message but not requiring feedback or comment.
- Consulting – this approach allows choice between predetermined options not an opportunity to propose alternatives.

- Deciding together – here views are shared, options generated jointly a course of action agreed upon.
- Acting together – parties are working with others to make decisions and carry through the action agreed.
- Supporting local initiatives – which involve supporting groups to develop and implement their own solutions.

This has been an influential view, some of which are reflected in current British government policy. For Britain's New Labour government, action to engage local communities has also been driven by the Civil Renewal agenda. This too is about government and people working together to make life better. Former Home Secretary, David Blunkett, set out his vision for civil renewal:[43]

> We must aim to build strong, empowered and active communities, in which people increasingly do things for themselves and the state acts to facilitate, support and enable citizens to lead self-determined, fulfilled lives. In this way, we will genuinely link the economic and social, the civil and formal political arena, the personal with the public realm.

The three essential ingredients of civil renewal expressed here are

- active citizenship
- strengthened communities
- partnership in meeting public needs

Community engagement becomes then the democratic process by which civil renewal is advanced. It operates at three corresponding levels:

- Enabling people to understand and exercise their powers and responsibilities as citizens.
- Empowering citizens to organize through groups in pursuit of their common good.
- Ensuring state bodies support the involvement of citizens in influencing and executing their public duties.

Engagement is the involvement of the public, either as individuals or as a community, in policy and service decisions that affect them. In practice, this involvement can take a number of different forms. From this government perspective, the three main forms of engagement are:

Information gathering   This involves the collection of information about public attitudes and requirements through surveys, and such like. There is no ongoing dialogue between the public and the organization seeking the information. Public participation here is largely with and by individuals.

Consultation   Here, members of the public and the organization work together for a defined period to discuss a particular policy or service issue. The methods used might range from focus groups to citizens' juries. People are brought together as representatives of the demographic profile of a particular community.

Participation   Members of the public and the organization work together, on an ongoing basis, on a range of policy or service issues. These tend to focus on the community rather than on individuals. Community forums are an example.

A key difference among these three kinds of engagement is the extent of the 'dialogue' that takes place, the exchange of views, ideas and concerns among different groups. The information-gathering approach does not involve much dialogue, whereas the participation approach is about continuous dialogue as part of joint working.

16   A different approach

An alternative model, a different way of looking at and linking these concepts, is pictured in Figure 7. It may help us to understand community engagement in a more developmental way, which in turn may be more helpful to schools, in particular, because it opens up some understanding of the educative role they can play in building community engagement.

This illustration suggests a model that can be viewed as a type of matrix. It works like this. The model recognizes and builds on those three broad approaches through which communities might be engaged, already discussed – information gathering, consultation and participation.

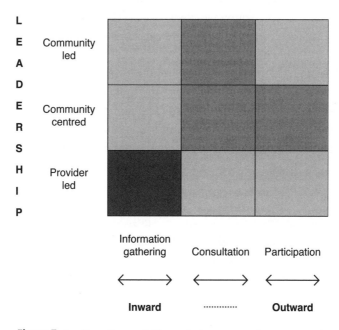

Figure 7 An alternative model for analysing community engagement.

Each of these three approaches can operate across a spectrum of engagement with the wider community, from being inward-looking towards myself or my group, moving towards looking out in the direction of others. For each of these three possible approaches, also, the role of leaders can be categorized by the approach they take. This might range from clear control and direction (provider led), through sharing greater responsibility and decision-making about the activity with participants (community centred), to facilitating the community in determining and managing their own activity (community led).

To illustrate, consider the relatively simple example of a youth club. In a provider-led approach, information gathering might involve the adult leaders in planning activities for the club, perhaps based on information they gather about what others do or say. Consultation at this level might include asking members of the youth club which of two options they want to do next week so as to guide the leaders in making a decision. Participation might involve some members in helping to organize the resulting activity.

Where there is a community-centred approach to leadership, some chosen young people might be working more directly alongside adult leaders to decide on the list of what activity the club's leaders should arrange for them. A community-centred leadership approach to participation could involve the members in some aspects of organizing the resulting activity, under a greater or lesser degree of supervision.

Engagement occurs most fully with the community-led approach to leadership. This might mean, for instance, the young people were directly putting together the options and taking responsibility for consulting about and carrying through that activity.

A traffic light approach to colouring the resulting types of activity, red (darker shade box in Figure 7), amber (medium shaded boxes in Figure 7), green (lighter-shaded boxes in Figure 7), can help to give an indication of direction and priority. It is key to understanding the model to recognize that work in all the nine boxes has a legitimate place. And each new generation within a community will require opportunities to gain experience across all areas of the grid. In other words, progression here is not simply about climbing a one-direction ladder.

But there is a clear progression in terms of skills and development through from the bottom left corner of the grid up towards the higher right-hand corner. And as engagement moves out of the red zone into amber and green zones, the role of leaders and educators begins to shift towards encouraging and enabling greater levels of responsibility and initiative, preparing, equipping and supporting that development. The role of the leader is moving towards being a facilitator, whose task is to act as a resource and also to help reflect on the development that takes place.

It is, therefore, possible to take any activity and locate it somewhere within the matrix. There is never an exact right place for any particular piece of work. Rather the model offers a tool for promoting discussion and thought about the intentions and priorities for the work, and, for a school, about the balance of the ways in which it works with its communities.

Successful community engagement is therefore judged, not just by the area or style of working in which an activity was carried out, but more especially by the rate and frequency at which people were enabled to progress through to the higher levels of engagement, from red zones, through amber and towards green-zone activity.

17 Finding a balance – the Shotton Hall experience

Progression, pace and purpose in community engagement are important. But, even in the best-planned and best-supported situations, it happens that not every good idea people have can be made to work. Not all plans succeed, and sometimes a change of course is required. Ian Mowbray, Headteacher of Shotton Hall School in Durham, recounts his experience of success in community engagement, and also of coming up against some of the limitations inherent in our present understanding of schools' roles.

Ian came to the headship of Shotton Hall, an 11–16 school in Peterlee's Easington District, one of the most deprived areas in Britain, in April 2001. Data were not particularly rich at this time, but all the indicators were there for anyone to see. Just over 1,000 students, a run-down site, a reception that resembled a public toilet, and a uniform of sweatshirt and trousers that had clearly seen better days. 'Peterlee – the place to be', the town council's strap line, clearly felt a misnomer for Ian. It didn't feel like the place to be and by the end of his first week, Ian knew it wasn't.

The school yard during lesson time, he recalls, resembled Oxford Street on a busy Saturday. More students were clearly out of lessons than in and behaviour was to say the least interesting. Many staff struggled to keep order and expectations were low. The 'canny bairn' syndrome prevailed. Low expectations were confirmed by that summer's GCSE results. Only 25.6 per cent of over 200 students achieved five A*–C grades. Attendance was running at just over 87 per cent and fixed-term exclusions were in the hundreds. Something had to give. There was absolutely nothing to lose, and this became the mantra and driving force that brought about radical change, and later some notable success.

In such a small close-knit community, Ian was surprised that the school had very little community involvement. A number of groups hired the sports hall, the gymnasium and the football pitch. There was, and indeed still is, a thriving 'Out of School Hours' group that provided childcare. Other than this, there was nothing. Ian, a long-time believer in the benefits of community development and community involvement, was certain that this had to change if the school was to make progress. He believed that people within the local community had to value what education offered and had to see the school as a centre of excellence, not a place that confirmed all of their worst prejudices. But before this could even begin to happen, the image of the school simply had to change.

September 2001 was a crucial month. Things had to be seen to be different. That summer the entire school was externally painted in corporate colours. New headed paper, a new strap line, 'Achievement through Partnership', a new uniform of blazer, badge and tie, and a whole host of feel-good stories in the local press, all had an impact. Social inclusion funds were used to overcome financial difficulties for many families in purchasing a uniform. A new code of behaviour was introduced with innovative rewards and clearly defined sanctions. A first bid for specialist status failed, but finally in 2002 the school was designated a Specialist Performing Arts College. People could almost taste the difference. The change in ethos was tangible, and the next year's examination results, although not brilliant by any stretch of the imagination, showed significant improvement. Thirty-seven per cent of all Year 11 students achieved five A*–C grades, fixed-term exclusions were halved and attendance was over 90 per cent.

At about this time a new science teacher was appointed. Ellen, a local woman, had worked in industry and at the local further education college. It turned out Ellen had also been very involved in a local voluntary organization called East Durham Partnership (EDP). The Partnership already provided a range of adult education courses with some degree of success. A certain synergy began to become apparent. The leader of the local Education Action Zone was very keen to support development at Shotton Hall, and the idea of seconding Ellen part-time to audit community provision formed. Ellen was well placed. She knew the area and she knew the key people. Again fortuitously, EDP had a link with a national voluntary body, the Community Action Network (CAN), and a meeting was arranged with CAN's CEO, Andrew Mawson. The meeting with Andrew was seminal. His ideas on an entrepreneurial community were at the time ground breaking, and together they began to see ways forward for the school to develop its community arm.

Within months the school was part of a vibrant national organization. Networking was bringing them into contact with a number of influential people, and meetings in London with a range of dynamic players in education and community development helped to formulate plans for the school. Ian says that:

> I can't pretend that for a quiet lad from the provinces this wasn't daunting. Indeed, I will never forget my first important meeting at CAN headquarters when I got lost on my way there. It was a scorching day and dressed in best city suit I pounded the streets of London trying to find the venue. Eventually successful, but one hour late for this incredibly important meeting, I arrived dripping in

perspiration. Before entering the meeting I visited the toilet to freshen up. I washed my face and dripping wet then discovered there were no towels. Toilet roll was the answer. Eagerly tearing pieces of toilet roll, I dried myself, adjusted my tie, and nervously entered one of the most important meetings of my life. People were kind and understanding but I couldn't help noticing them strangely looking at me. Meeting over and having survived this ordeal I once more visited the toilet before setting out to board the train home. Imagine my horror when I looked in the mirror and saw three pieces of toilet tissue attached to my brow. If the ground could have opened up . . .

In May 2002, on the day Office for Standards in Education arrived for a full inspection of the school, EDP was moving onto the site, with a full meeting of the now burgeoning community development team planned. Ian thought of cancelling all this to concentrate on the inspection. But time was of the essence.

In hindsight the registered inspector attending this two hour meeting was actually a positive thing. At the time, quite frankly, it was scary! Imagine a relatively new Head Teacher, a Government Minister, local dignitaries, a registered inspector with her whole team on site, and a whole voluntary organisation with its UK On-line Centre and its staff all moving on to the site on the same day!

Nevertheless, all went well. The inspection, while not brilliant, recognized the progress being made, and an intense week became a crucial cornerstone in the school's development. EDP hit the ground running. Adult learners became a part and parcel of Shotton Hall School life. Parenting groups, courses for the unemployed, Helping Hands, Football in the Community and a whole host of other community-based activities helped to establish the school at the heart of its community.

The capital project for the new specialism was a dance studio and before long a new, state-of-the-art dance studio was being built, with sprung floor and mirrored walls. Other developments continued to move quickly. The Chair of EDP became a school governor, and community development was enshrined as one of the school's core objectives. CAN continued to support the school. BBC Radio 4 made a half-an-hour documentary about the school entitled *Changing Places*. BBC television did a feature on its local news programme *Look North*. DEMOS, the national policy think tank, conducted some very positive research about the school and its community. Government ministers, the DFES Innovation Unit and civil servants, all visited the school, and were seemingly interested in developments.

As these events unfolded, the school continued to prosper. Results at both key stages continued to improve and other statistics relating to attendance and fixed-term exclusions continued to impress.

For a long time, it felt to those involved like an exciting and positively charged roller coaster ride. EDP went from strength to strength, as did the school. There was a strong sense of mutual benefit, and all seemed to be winners. Within months, a community library, a community classroom, a teenage referral centre, a brand new school and community technology village were on site. Peterlee, and more specifically Shotton Hall School, *was* 'the place to be'. It felt vibrant, and as if the school and its community were coming together.

The school's specialism in Performing Arts enabled it to develop outreach community work in local primary schools. The school employed a community arts co-ordinator, an actor in residence, a brass tutor, a singing coach and a dance coach to help to develop the performing arts in local primary and secondary schools. From a position of having virtually no performance groups, there are now three steel bands, an orchestra, a brass band and three choirs. The performing arts are alive and well in Peterlee. The annual Cultural Heritage Week hosted at the school, which involves upwards of 800 young people, is living proof of this.

The performance of the school with regard to public examinations has improved year on year. In 2007, 57 per cent of all Year 11 students achieved five A*–C grades, and at Key Stage 3 the school matched or exceeded national averages for level five grades in English, Mathematics and Science. It has been no miracle. Growth and improvement have been both organic and systematic. But Ian Mowbray remains convinced that the community engagement programme was seminal in supporting these improvements.

Over this period, EDP has continued to flourish. Its community schemes, and its factory refurbishing furniture, have provided much-needed local employment and at the same time helped to regenerate the area. Ellen is now part-time Head of Health and Social Care at school and Chief Executive of EDP. The Partnership has moved to new premises off the school site, and its chair is no longer a school governor. This split was not acrimonious but perhaps needed to happen, which is where this story all becomes rather interesting.

During the period of exciting partnership between Shotton Hall School (the public sector) and EDP (the voluntary sector), anything seemed possible. With the help of the local Primary Care Trust and the Local Authority, they collectively developed a scheme for a Life Park on the school site. This imaginative scheme seemed to all of them to match local regeneration plans and also cover the 'Every Child Matters' agenda through a whole range of public, private and voluntary sector agencies all working on the same site. Building Schools for the Future (BSF) would combine with other public and private funding to develop a park on which children's services, health, social services and private enterprise would all combine to produce truly 'joined-up' services. The plans were well received, but in hindsight Ian believes this is when things began to deteriorate.

The truth would seem to be that different sectors work in different ways. Access to funding and the use of that funding are very different, for example, in the voluntary sector compared to the public sector. There had already been signs of a tension developing in school. EDP could access and use funds that the school simply could not. EDP could get jobs done more quickly, more directly. EDP was allowed greater freedom to purchase and extend than any public organization. While it was clear that joint ventures would produce dynamic, even scintillating results, the public sector's restrictions were often a barrier.

The Life Park was simply a step too far. Without the total backing and drive of a major player, such as the Local Authority or the Primary Care Trust, it became clear that EDP and the school could not really pursue this dream. Local reorganization, regulations pertaining to land ownership and the absolute clear need for someone with real power to lead the development, all combined to prevent the dream from becoming a reality. It seemed that everyone loved the idea, saw its logic, but nobody was really prepared to take it on. There were quite simply too many barriers and too many 'what ifs'.

The dynamic relationship between the voluntary sector and the public sector that had burned so brightly had begun to lose its impact. EDP began to develop increasingly as a force for good in the community, and the school began to focus more directly on teaching and learning. The two organizations began to move in different directions that were not necessarily complementary. No one person or event was responsible for this. Nevertheless, the moment of opportunity was lost. A dream of real community empowerment by a planned and strategic partnership between the voluntary and public sectors evaporated. With it went the opportunity to direct various resources in combination to create lifelong learning opportunities and a very real sense of community cohesion. No one was to blame, except perhaps 'the system'. A system that they found lacked flexibility and dynamism. A system that turns slowly, like some huge tanker, is not a system easily able to respond to modern educational and community needs. The needs of both sectors can be addressed with 'joined-up' thinking and flexibility, but that means tackling the monolith of a system designed many, many moons ago for a very different world.

Both Shotton Hall School and EDP achieved success, sometimes mutually and sometimes exclusively. When there was mutual success, it felt to those involved that anything was possible. But, and it's a very big 'but', they now tend to feel that present statutory, regulatory and financial systems in England actively find it to hard to cope with entrepreneurial thinking and action, and consequently create a tendency to subjugate creative thinking to the realm of the impossible.

That is a pity because the story of Shotton Hall offers both important encouragement and some important warnings. It is highly significant that, like other schools cited in this book, its commitment to community engagement was not at the expense of its commitment to raising standards. Although there is no objective research evidence to connect the two, those on the ground believe that latter would not have happened without the former. And there are now a growing number of situations, nationally and internationally, where that feeling is taking hold for the long term.

At the same time, there can be dangers to the success of the school in its core purposes if external influences try to tip the balance too quickly and too far. As a result, Shotton Hall had to find a new equilibrium between the two. And it managed to do that, albeit not without some painful rethinking. In achieving that change, their story highlights the need for every school to continually reflect carefully about the pace and purpose of its development.

18   Working with networks

One reason why the more fluid approach of the nine-box model, with its emphasis on a developmental rather than a straight-line approach, may be more helpful in understanding the connection between schooling and community engagement is because the world is increasingly not organized along the lines of simple models. Our understanding of the nature of organizations, and indeed societies, has been significantly changed and enhanced by our growing understanding of the importance of and nature of networks, and of network analysis theory.

One of the key movers in this development is Professor Karen Stephenson, who came to management theory after studying the fine arts, anthropology and chemistry. According to Art Kleiner, 'she talks about organisations as if they were still-lifes, researches them as if they were tribes, and plots their decisions as if they were chemical reactions. She is simultaneously a management academic (teaching at Harvard's School of Design and Imperial College's School of Management at the University of London), a computer software entrepreneur (her company, NetForm International, holds the patents on a set of software algorithms for analysing human networks) and a consultant on the nature of networks in large organisations, particularly as vehicles for change'.[44]

To Karen Stephenson, the association between trust and learning is an instrument of vast, if frequently untapped, organizational power. The act of reconnecting and talking with a trusted colleague generally triggers a resurgence of mutual memory, opening the gates to fresh learning and invention. This phenomenon, she contends, is just one example of the direct cognitive connection between the amount of trust in an organization and its members' ability to develop and deploy tacit knowledge together. Because networks of trust release so much cognitive capability, they can (and often do) have far more influence over the fortunes and failures of an organization, from day to day and year to year, than the official hierarchy.

This concept, which she calls the 'quantum theory of trust', explains not just how to recognize the collective cognitive capability of organizations, but how to cultivate and increase it.[45] Professor Stephenson's work has perhaps come to seem less counter-intuitive recently. An organization like Al Qaeda has demonstrated just how powerful informal connections can be. There is the growing awareness that ideas and trends, like epidemics, spread in non-linear manner, with the makeup of human contact being the most important factor, the insight pinpointed by Malcolm Gladwell in his bestseller *The Tipping Point*.[46]

Karen Stephenson doesn't suggest replacing hierarchies with networks. Rather, she sees organizations as a sort of double-helix system, with hierarchy and networks perpetually influencing each other, ideally co-evolving over time to become more effective. In any culture, she believes, there are at least six core layers of knowledge, each with its own informal network of people exchanging conversation, shown in Figure 8. Everybody moves in all the networks, but different people play different roles in each; a hub in one may be a gatekeeper in another.

1. The Work Network. (With whom do you exchange information as part of your daily work routines?) The everyday contacts of routine operations represent the habitual, mundane 'resting pulse' of a culture. 'The functions and dysfunctions; the favours and flaws always become evident here', says Professor Stephenson.

2. The Social Network. (With whom do you 'check in', inside and outside work, to find out what is going on?) This is important primarily as an indicator of the trust within a culture. Healthy organizations are those whose numbers fall within a normative range, with enough social 'tensile strength' to withstand stress and uncertainty, but not so much that they are overdemanding of people's personal time and invested social capital.

3. The Innovation Network. (With whom do you collaborate or kick around new ideas?) There is a guilelessness and childlike wonderment to conversations conducted in this network, as people talk openly about their perceptions, ideas and experiments. For instance, 'Why do we use four separate assembly lines where three would do?' Or, 'Hey, let's try it and see what happens!' Key people in this network take a dim view of tradition and may clash with the keepers of corporate lore and expertise, dismissing them as relics.

4. The Expert Knowledge Network. (To whom do you turn for expertise or advice?) Organizations have core networks, whose key members hold the critical and established, yet tacit, knowledge of the enterprise. Like the Coca-Cola formula, this kind of knowledge is frequently kept secret. Key people in this network are often threatened by innovation; they're likely to clash with innovators and think of them as 'undisciplined'.

5. The Career Guidance or Strategic Network. (Whom do you go to for advice about the future?) If people tend to rely on others in the same company for mentoring and career guidance, then that in itself indicates a high level of trust. This network often directly influences corporate strategy; both decisions about careers and strategic moves, after all, are focused on the future.

6. The Learning Network. (Whom do you work with to improve existing processes or methods?) Key people in this network may end up as bridges between hubs in the expert and innovation networks, translating between the old guard and the new. Since most people are afraid of genuine change, this network tends to lie dormant until the change awakens a renewed sense of trust. 'It takes a tough kind of love', says Professor Stephenson, 'to entrust people to tell you what they know about your established habits, rules, and practices'.

Figure 8   Karen Stephenson's six networks.
Source: Kleiner, A. *Strategy and Business* (24 November 2006).

19 Searching together for the future

A school which is working on engaging with its communities will need to study, understand, build and work through networks, such as those outlined by Karen Stephenson. Hierarchical or bureaucratic approaches to representative structures will not succeed in drawing people in. The experience of Oakgrove School, described in Section 4 (Build . . .), highlights the importance of 'structured informality'.

Two Americans, Sandra Janoff and Marvin Weissbord, have developed a very interesting and interactive technique, called Future Search, which a number of schools in England have now begun to use to build non-bureaucratic community engagement around key issues of common concern.[47]

In a Future Search, participants seek to take that first important step by

- getting the 'whole system' in the room
- creating a learning environment for participants to experience the whole system
- searching for common ground from which to build action plans
- asking individuals to take responsibility to act on the common ground articulated

The change begins in the planning. Future Search requires no training, inputs, data collection or diagnoses. People face each other, rather than concepts, expert advice or assumptions about what they lack and should do. The method involves comparing notes and listening, sometimes to a mishmash of assumptions, misinformation, stereotypes and judgements rattling around in all of us. Amazingly, it is not necessary to straighten all this out to succeed. Commitment builds as the group encounter chaos together, hang on despite anxiety, and come out of the other side with some good ideas, people they can trust and faith in their ability to work together.

In 2004, Bolton, like all other local authorities in England, was trying to find a way to pull their services together into a Children's Services Department. It was said that the three core services – education, social services and health – had a different culture, and certainly had very different processes. There was significant anxiety about the impact on people's work and these different ways of dealing with things such as client confidentiality. Moreover, whereas schools predominantly provided a universal service and worked much at the levels of initial support and intervention, social services dealt with clients in difficulty and at serious risk. The council also had to think not just about these services but also about how to reorganize the whole local provision. So in any move to Children's Services, what, for instance, would happen to the adult part of care? And what would happen to that part of the education service that has to do with adult education and leisure?

For this bigger process, the council followed a typical route of bringing in an external consultancy firm. However, the Future Search approach sought to achieve something else – a commonality of purpose and a chance to work together to solve the problem.

Bringing the whole system together meant including everyone that worked with or was involved in services to young people as recipients, carers or providers. Nine stakeholder groups, each comprising nine representatives, were invited. This included parents/carers, two groups of young people, teachers, social care teams, police and security services, and voluntary services. This balance was important because there are opportunities to work as a group, and times when mixed groups had a representative of each sector. They had to cover every aspect of the town's population. So it would have been totally inappropriate to have just high-achieving articulate learners. You also had to have those with 'a bit of a history', or excluded from schools and in a referral unit. There had to be a mix of parents/carers and a balance that represented the full heritage mix of the town. Not to have included a section of the population, however challenging the engagement might be, would weaken the argument that 'the whole system was in the room'. So you found the Executive Member for Education and the Director in a group that included a young person who was looked after by the council. The whole system had to be there together.

And, together, they explored the past and identified the things that they were pleased to have done and the things they were sorry about. It quickly became clear that the issues young people face to day had a resonance with everyone when they were at school. This developed an ownership of the issues. Participants shared their understanding of the present and produced a huge mind map of the key issues facing young people in the town. They then elected to work in mixed groups to outline some ways forward for these mind-map themes.

The group moved on to what they would like to see in the future to ensure that every child in Bolton mattered. They described the community they would create and the values held. They described the programmes that would be in place and how relationships would be managed. They thought about the biggest barriers they would have to overcome and how these could be overcome. The whole group then built up a picture of what they agreed with and where there was still some disagreement. Where there was consensus, key stakeholders then undertook to take some action over the next year when a review day would take place.

What was surprising about this Future Search was the large degree of consensus and the positive relationships that were built up during it. But another key feature was the involvement of young people. They played a significant part in the organization and planning of the day. They hosted it, they brought it to a conclusion and they established a blog so people could continue to develop their ideas. It was in the end about them!

Three days was a tremendous commitment for people to make in terms of time. But there may be other ways that some of the techniques and principles can be used without such a great commitment of time. The model can be scaled so schools can use the technique to find a collaborative vision of the way forward and build a focus for their community engagement.

Too many schools start off with bright ideas and enthusiasm for their community role, which then falters through a lack of connection. A regenerating school gives the community the power to identify the future they desire and to which the school can then respond with confidence and in partnership. Future Search principles may offer one tool to help bring that about.

Janoff and Weissbord sum up as follows:

> A Future Search enables us to experience and accept polarities. It helps us learn how to bridge barriers of culture, class, age, gender, ethnicity, power structures and hierarchy by working as peers on tasks of mutual concern. It interrupts our tendency to repeat old patterns and gives us a chance to express our highest ideals. Instead of trying to change the world or each other, we change the conditions under which we interact. That much we can control, and changing the conditions leads to surprising outcomes.

20 Growing listening wrinkles

Debra Jacobs is the Chief Librarian of Seattle Public Library in the US with a fierce commitment to community engagement in the slightly different context of leading a public library service. She has pursued community engagement to the extent of persuading her community to raise a special tax, or bond issue, to build a stunning brand new central library and a library in every community. Debra describes this as 'their gift to themselves'. What is the essence of community engagement for her?

> One of my leadership 'aha' moments was realising the importance of treating each person and each organisation as a unique organisation. When I speak to people in what we here call nursing homes; their needs are different and in an ethical way I know what their needs are, I talk to them differently than when I talk to the Rotary Club: that has different kinds of needs . . . so I have to show them what the need is. That means doing your homework, knowing who your collaborator might be, whether it's a health professional or whatever, and thinking 'What can I do with them?'

> Soon after I moved to Seattle ten years ago, a neighbourhood activist came up to me, touched me on my brow. She pointed to her forehead, and she said 'That wrinkle there; that's why you're so popular'. And I said 'What are you talking about?' He replied, 'That's your listening wrinkle, because you listen totally to who is talking to you'.[48]

The regenerating school has lots of listening wrinkles too. That's because, through conscious intent, clear purpose and careful planning, it's become very good at developing community engagement.

Change Study 3
Caroline Springs Community College, Victoria, Australia

www.carolinesprings.vic.edu.au

Gabrielle Leigh

Gabrielle Leigh joined the Caroline Springs Education Services Group in 2000 when she was appointed as Principal of the Government school, at that stage catering for students from P through to Year 6. She is now College Director of Caroline Springs College – a multi-campus Kindergarten to Year 12 College, and has helped to lead the project through concept development to full implementation.

IMAGINE a twenty-first-century learning community, based on new forms of ownership and structures for delivery, committed to building a culture of lifelong learning . . .

On a basalt plain 22 kilometres west of Melbourne, in the state of Victoria, Australia, lies a new housing estate with a ground-breaking educational complex at its core. The Caroline Springs development has been established within an innovative framework. Planning for this greenfield site has been, and continues to be, extensive.

The largest education provider on site, Caroline Springs College, is challenging the status quo in education delivery. The College is Victoria's only Kindergarten to Year 12 government school and is situated in a rapidly growing community on the urban fringe.

Delfin Lendlease, the land developer, organized a forum for school planners from government, catholic and independent divisions to meet with a range of people including the local Shire of Melton. The rationale was to investigate the opportunity to create a new model in education delivery. Following this discussion in 1997, the Caroline Springs Education Services Working Party was established to devise plans and strategies for future development. This group consisted of academics, business people, community representatives and school providers. Support in the concept development came from Delfin Lendlease Property developers, who have established a community perspective in real estate development throughout Australia. The intention was to build a number of schools from different sectors in education to act as the fulcrum and centre for a new community. These education providers were brought to the table to plan together with the local shire.

In 1997, before a sod of land was turned, the Caroline Springs Education Services Working Party identified the following attributes for a twenty-first-century learning community:

- A commitment to exploring new forms of ownership with a philosophy of sharing and collaboration among educational providers.
- A commitment to exploring new structures in the provision of education services.
- A commitment to lifelong learning.

With this orientation and direction established prior to any organizational building, there was a philosophical framework to plan for the future.

This change study looks at the implementation of these three attributes in line with the development of an innovative structure for the students of Caroline Springs College and the wider community.

1. A commitment to exploring new forms of ownership and structures with a philosophy of sharing and collaboration among educational providers

Caroline Springs College has been formed as a multi-campus institution. The underlying aim is to provide a seamless education to assist in the pursuit of lifelong learning. There are three Kindergarten to Year 9 campuses: The Brookside Campus, The Creekside Campus and Springside Campus. Lakeview Later Years is a Year 10–12 campus. Each campus has its own distinct signature made explicit by specific strategic alliances with the local community. However, there is strong connectivity to the whole structure with leaders and staff working purposefully across campuses to share learning and resources to fulfill the aims of the College. The water theme flows throughout Caroline Springs.

a. Brookside Campus

The Brookside Campus, which opened in 2000, is one of three schools that comprise 'The Brookside Learning Centre', and was the first educational facility in the area. The Brookside Learning Centre includes Mowbray College, an independent college, Christ the Priest Catholic Primary School, a child-minding centre, a maternal and child health centre, a preschool centre, Djerriwarrh Health services and the Local Learning Employment Network (LLEN). A number of facilities are shared between Caroline Springs College and Mowbray College, including the reception and administration area, staffroom, library, arts facilities, meeting rooms, gymnasium, and sports and recreation areas. Other facilities and grounds are shared with the Shire of Melton and the Western Jets Football Club. This could not succeed without a mutual philosophy of sharing and collaboration among all educational providers.

Another example of real collaboration on the ground occurred in 2004 when the government school grew faster than anticipated and needed land to house students. Due to the relationship on the ground between the two principals, the Catholic division made land available for short-term additional facilities for government students. Now that is a first!

b. Creekside Campus

The Creekside Campus, the College's second campus, opened in 2005 for Kindergarten to Year 9. The Melton Shire has a close partnership with the College and built on college land to create a preschool, maternal and childcare, toy library and occasional care, all incorporated as part of the site. The College has opted to deliver the preschool education. The collaboration goes further as it reflects a whole of government approach to education and childcare. Within 2 years, the Kindergarten is now considered an integral part of the school and its planning in learning and teaching approaches is embedded within the College structure. Equally the thorough lines of curriculum are being written to ensure continuity, consistency and strength as each child progresses through the specific stages of learning.

c. Lakeview Later Years Campus

Lakeview Later Years Campus caters for Years 10–12 and opened in 2006 at the Town Centre. Lakeview provides students with specific pathways in Victorian Certificate of Education (VCE), Victorian Certificate of Applied Learning (VCAL) and Vocational Education and Training (VET) courses. This structure caters for academic and technical streams. Students from the other campuses feed into Lakeview. This campus has a large performing arts theatre facility. Due to an innovative approach of ownership and sharing, which is a specific characteristic of the Caroline Springs development, this facility was doubled in seating and is open for community use outside school hours, reinforcing the notion of lifelong learning.

As part of this campus development, the College has contributed allocated funds towards the building of the municipal library rather than creating its own library. In this 'state-of-the-art' Library, there is a designated IT facility available for students of Caroline Springs College throughout the day, and the book collection is extensive. The College Director is based in this facility, reinforcing the concept of education being at the centre of the community development.

Another example of sharing innovation is found in the large indoor court municipal sport and recreation facility. Again Caroline Springs College and Mowbray College have contributed to the construction and will have full school-time access to at least one of the basketball courts. In turn the community will use this after school hours. The Shire of Melton administers this facility and the schools contribute to the management and servicing.

Due to all these high levels of collaboration, college students have enhanced facilities for their education.

d. Springside Campus

Springside Campus will open in 2009 as a Kindergarten to Year 9 complex. This campus has established strategic sharing arrangements with Melton Shire to provide a preschool, maternal and childcare, toy library and occasional care as part of the site. Adjacent are

Shire ovals, which will be used by the college students. On the education site, a catholic school and an independent college are being developed simultaneously. There is a Memorandum of Understanding to assist in the development of the site as a whole. It seeks to develop trust and understanding across the three educational sectors. Government, Independent and Catholic educators are currently working together to give the new community real choices while having optimum access to a range of facilities.

There are few multi-campus schools in the government sector in Victoria. However Caroline Springs, as a four-campus Kindergarten to Year 12 provider has been created to address the specific development needs in a brand new community. The delivery of government education for a significant cohort of students, 3,500 of them by 2010, is consistent across all campuses and enhanced due to the innovative sharing inherent in the structures.

2. A commitment to exploring new structures in the provision of education services within Caroline Springs College

The configuration of the college is outside the mould of traditional education structures. The Victorian Government was supportive of the plans of the Caroline Springs College Council in setting up a new configuration in schooling in the west of Melbourne. The students come from lower socio-economic groups and may not have as many pathways open to them as students from the leafy green suburbs in the east of Melbourne. There are over 54 nationalities within this growing culture. There was a real need to imagine an improved structure and give added opportunities to the learners.

The structure, when it was established, was quite unique. It broke the traditional Primary and Secondary division creating a progressive learning environment. The actual configuration of the Caroline Springs College has been shaped to suit the learning needs of the students and to establish collaboration between teachers and community members. This is a result of extensive research and planning into the specific learning needs of students.

Traditionally, Victorian government schools have been organized into Primary Prep–Year 6 and Secondary Year 7–12 configuration. Kindergartens or preschools have sat outside education. This organization evolved from the industrial era of the early twentieth century. The division between primary and secondary gave a clear separation, which suited the structured era when boundaries were not blurred. No longer does the world look remotely like the early twentieth-century environment – so why are schools still rigidly configured in that manner that was suited to that bygone age?

After extensive research, the organizational structures of K–9 educational facilities were decided upon. The reasons were extensive. Some are listed below:

- A reduced number of transition points for students.
- Ease of collaboration between staff and planning is consistent within stages of education – early, middle and later years.
- Added expertise of educators coming from traditional primary and secondary backgrounds.
- Organizationally, leaders and teams are structured around specific learning needs inherent in the specific stage of education.

The students most at risk are found within the middle years of learning, Years 5–9. With the advent of preadolescence, it is even more important for the school environment to be specifically designed around the needs of adolescent learners. Learning can be divided into reasonable chunks, which can be targeted towards specific learning requirements for individuals, with a focus on personalized pedagogy. This can result in a rich learning environment designed for a tailor-made curriculum.

Some of the immediate outcomes at Caroline Springs College are the following:

- Leadership in Year 9 with coaching roles helping the social development in leadership for older students.
- Special assistance in primary programmes with cross age tutoring and mentoring.
- Active Student Voice in the design, implementation and evaluation of curriculum.
- Extra resources available across the whole school.
- Planning across the Early Years/Middle Years/Later Years results in high-level expertise across areas.
- Curriculum development from Kindergarten to Year 12, with consistency across early, middle and later years.
- All students and staff understand the structure, and the same mission and values accepted in early years are sustained throughout all the years of schooling.

3. A commitment to lifelong learning

Each provider deliberated on how they could deliver lifelong learning to their community. In 2000, the year of opening, Caroline Springs College discussed and established its mission and specific college values. These have served to give a unified direction for the development and building of the four campuses. The college has eight key values to underpin its commitment to delivering World Class Learning within a global context. These values are consistent and live within the students over the year of Kindergarten and the 13 years of formal education. They are *Lifelong Learning, Happiness, Respect, Achievement, Knowledge, Responsibility, Teamwork* and *Community*. The meaning of community has helped in the planning and building of social capital within Caroline Springs. It is defined as sharing and supporting a common context, purpose and/or learning environment aiming at making a difference for our students.

The value of Lifelong Learning is in harmony with the initial intent of Caroline Springs Education Services Group. Consistency flowed from the planning process into the actual school operation. Much discussion ensued as to what Lifelong Learning might mean to the new community of 72 students and parents, and also how it might endure over time. Thirty-five parents and all the teachers of Caroline Springs College agreed the explicit meaning in 2000. Lifelong Learning was perceived as a strong commitment to continuous learning and self-development. Over subsequent years this value has been embedded into the prevailing culture. It fits well with the innovation of the education site and it defines each person in the Caroline Springs College community as a learner for life.

As the founding principal of Caroline Springs College, a Victorian Government School, Gabrielle Leigh had the responsibility to help create a learning environment that broke the mould. It was a rare opportunity to imagine what is possible in education, to question the existing replication of traditional delivery models and create pathways for the future. At each stage, student learning needed to be the prime focus, at the centre of all decision-making processes. As College Director, her role has been consistent and has withstood the passage of time. The Leadership team has worked hard to create high-level innovative learning opportunities across each campus.

The underlying goal was to keep focused on implementing the values and mission. At Caroline Springs College, this meant to promote the lifelong development and growth of students, so that they achieve their fullest potential as individuals and as members of a healthy local community and an international society, reflected in the mission statement – World Class Learning.

Conclusion

In developing strategic partnerships among all members of the Caroline Springs community the focus of the college is to improve:

- student learning
- student engagement and well-being
- student pathways and transition

All members of the school community are committed to providing an optimum learning environment. The high-level planning occurring at every stage in the development has directly contributed to increased academic opportunities for all students.

Despite extreme growth, with the student cohort increasing from 72 to 2,400 in 8 years, there has been no compromise in the standards of which the College is justifiably proud. In 2007, the College won a National Literacy Award in Early Years Education, and gained Council of International Schools (CIAS) accreditation in 2006.

Section 4
Build . . .

We understand and plan in order to be better able to build our dreams. That is only in part about building physical structures, though they are important. It is also about transforming the culture of what happens in and through a building. In England at this time we have an unprecedented opportunity to do both through the Building Schools for the Future Programme (BSF).

21 You can get it if you really want

The government commitment of around £3 billion year on year to rebuild every secondary school in England over 10–15 years represents a serious challenge to everyone involved in education. It is an opportunity for which, if it were to fail to have a transforming impact, all involved should be held to account.

Yet with the programme just in its earliest stages at the time of writing, some cynics were already speaking of their experience of it as Building Schools for the Present. How could this be, and more pertinently here, how can we make sure the schools we rebuild do really have the capability for regeneration? For no matter how state-of-the-art new buildings might be, no matter how well resourced they are, no matter how much leading-edge technology is packed inside, unless what happens inside them changes in some significant ways, there will be only limited change in the outcomes they produce.

Let's start with the physical building. There are two key problems for school building projects to overcome. To an extent they link. First, there is the innate tendency of all bureaucracies, working on a massive scale, to seek simplicity and readily understandable and transferable solutions. The second is the equally inevitable pressure to short circuit the processes, not just in terms of time, but more particularly by failing to take time to engage communities in thinking about the schools they want and need. A more detailed examination of procurement processes shows how problems can arise.

Stephen Forster was responsible, between 2004 and 2007, for managing secondary school transformation for Peterborough City Council. This included the closure of five schools in July 2007, opening a new Academy for 2,200 students in September 2007, at a cost of £47 million, implementing a £68 million scheme under the Private Finance Initiative (PFI) to refurbish and enlarge two schools and construct one new school for 1,675 students, as well as upgrading two Voluntary Aided schools and one Foundation school through Targeted Capital grants worth £30 million.

He, therefore, has a sharp insight into the many ways in which school buildings come to be renewed, extended or refurbished, as well as the many different drivers that lie behind each development, with many different interest groups, each with its own more or less effective lobbying process, trying to influence the design of the building, its detailed function and its availability. At each stage, new factors combine to press towards a lower common denominator.

In Stephen's experience, the key driver often reverts to a form of pragmatism, however, that may be dressed up through 'strategic' plans for an individual school, area or whole Local Authority. This pragmatism may be founded on 'basic need', the former category used by government to allocate capital resources when the number of children requiring a school place in an area significantly exceeded the number of places available. Or the pragmatism may reflect the condition of existing buildings, when it really is becoming impossibly expensive to keep patching them up.

Major new government initiatives, such as the Academies programme, can be accompanied by significant new capital funding for those prepared to realign their strategic direction sufficiently to meet the funding requirements. And for a capital-poor local authority, with major rebuilding needs in the foreseeable future, this may be the logical pragmatic response. There may also be a pragmatic response to the situation if a school or authority finds itself in a relatively generous funding position for some reason (planned or unplanned), and so takes the 'obvious' course of turning the hard cash into bricks and mortar, with the justification (not necessarily flawed) that improving the environment and facilities will have an impact on standards of achievement and attainment. This route is particularly available to Governing Bodies of Foundation, Aided or Trust Schools.

Therefore, in Stephen's view, before considering the impact of different procurement strategies for capital programmes, particularly PFI in its various phases and now BSF, it is important to recognize that this disjointed and pragmatic approach to building new school facilities inherently militate against the strategic and long-term thinking and planning needed to ensure that schools fit into some form of 'jigsaw', where each plays its part in promoting the regeneration of its local community through access to learning and skill opportunities, and social networking.

Most English secondary schools, especially specialist schools as we saw in Section 2 (Understand . . .), do now espouse the idea that they should take some steps to encourage and facilitate community involvement through extended access to their building, resources and expertise of their staff. Although such engagement may run through a school's ethos, aims and objectives, and may result in steps towards providing facilities for community use (even as a Phase 2 model of development), unless those principles underpin the strategic design and development of the building stock at every stage, the process is likely to produce obstacles, of varying complexity, to the effective implementation and management of a comprehensive community development and regeneration programme.

All uses of a school building, whether during the day, or in the evening, weekend or holiday periods, need to major on security, easy access to the provision of appropriate facilities and easily implemented systems to minimize costs (such as zoning heating systems). However, without the strongest community-aware ethos, such matters are not always at the front of the mind of the senior staff and governors, or Local Authority officers, when they are specifying a building and trying to procure it at the best possible value for money. Heating zones are relatively easy and cheap to include at the design stage of a new school, but can be very expensive to implement in the refurbishment of a building. Secure access to a school building, with a manned reception, may be placed some distance away from many of the facilities a community might wish to access, and along a complicated route, resulting in very difficult or very expensive to manage security issues within the building.

So a governing body with limited funding and a perceived resources problem may inevitably be tempted to build an extension to its school at the position perceived to be of most value during what is currently deemed 'the school day', or in the site which involves the least cost, rather than in the setting that gives the easiest and most functional access to the wider community. In the case of some of the harder decisions, it will take a very strong ethos of community engagement if that is to be the strongest factor. A simplistic example illustrating the difficulties governors and senior staff face might be the question of building a small classroom block but with one less classroom to allow space for community use. Should it go in a more difficult site in building terms but one that gives better community access, perhaps including during daytime? Given the nature of statutory responsibilities laid on governors, it may be very hard for them in such circumstances to prefer a solution that provides less new teaching space now, even though the longer term benefits may be greater.

In addition to potential conflict over priorities in building design at the local level, there is considerable potential for further conflict in the management of new and refurbished buildings if the designs do not take early account of, and attempt to reconcile, the needs and requirements of the different stakeholders. In particular, teaching staff and support staff who occupy buildings throughout the school day may take the view that the building is 'theirs'. It takes a strong ethos of outreach and community engagement, combined with effective liaison and partnership working, to overcome the disadvantages as these 'daytime' staff seek to personalize and 'own' their work areas.

Current and recent school building procurement processes, especially when inexpertly applied, as was the case with many of the earlier PFI schemes in England, can reinforce boundaries, and make integration and partnership working for the benefit of the community very difficult or indeed impossible.

The key stages of procurement begin with the Outline Business Case (OBC), which government representatives must approve if funding is to be released at all. This has to meet key requirements, including strict limits on floor areas and building costs, unless additional funding can be identified and confirmed at this early stage by the Local Authority. It is possible, by careful management of the available space, to create rooms that can have a community focus, but that will probably happen at the expense of total curriculum space, leading to an inevitable focus on what the priorities of the new school really are, unless the school has thought carefully about its curriculum and the need to link learning and life much more closely.

Although no concrete has been poured until long after the OBC is approved, it can feel as if, practically speaking, it is impossible to change the balance of accommodation later. Once the OBC is agreed, the Invitation to Negotiate (ITN) becomes the standard by which tenders will be judged, and that has to be firmly based on the OBC. The organizations that decide to submit a tender will have considerable discussion with both the Local Authority and the school representatives. But, at this stage, especially in the case of a new school, these school representatives may consist only of a new and inexperienced Temporary Governing Body. Only really visionary Local Authorities appoint a headteacher far enough in advance of the opening of a new school to have a real involvement in procurement. Even in an established school, it is quite common for neither governors nor headteacher to have had previous experience of capital procurement on this scale.

Potential builders will note the community ambitions and preferences of the school, but, ultimately, they have to submit a tender which will meet the specifications in the ITN at close to, if not actually at, the lowest price. Therefore, unless they have imaginative architects, the design of a building to enrich the local community may be far down their list of priorities.

Once the Preferred Bidder is determined, both they and the Local Authority then become enmeshed in the complex detail of contract negotiations, as strenuous efforts are made to close the contract not too long after building work has actually started. This adds another layer of difficult bureaucracy as details of the school's relationship with the Facilities Management (FM) provider in the successful consortium are worked out and defined in every detail for the next 25 years or so. Hours when the school building will be open, which parts can be accessed and the costs that will be charged for the use of different facilities at different times are recorded and agreed in fine detail. If, at this stage, the school ethos of community engagement is not clearly articulated, and enforced (and there may be significant funding issues attached to this), then the FM contract will act as a restraint on the comprehensive use of the facilities, and it will be next to impossible to undo the damage for the whole period of the contract.

In summary, therefore, the Governing Body and senior staff involved in procuring a new school through PFI or BSF, even under the more recent 'simplified' structure, must have a very clear and well-defined ethos which places community renewal and regeneration at the heart of their thinking, if the resulting building is to contribute to that end. They need to maintain this throughout all the difficult decisions they will have to make when their ambitions exceed the resources available. And unless the Local Authority are also prepared to support for aspiration, even when there are difficult funding and management issues to overcome, current procurement processes will tend to militate against any arrangement other than a conventional structure of daytime school, with some evening access to community facilities, where the FM services provider, with the explicit intention of generating profit, so chooses.

This is, of course, some way from the idea of a fully integrated community facility with emphasis on enriching and empowering the residents of the school locality. That requires a broader view, and some significant rethinking about the nature and purpose of public–private partnership that now underpins much public sector investment. This new thinking has to move beyond dominant and simplistic models of the purchaser–provider split towards concepts of joint social enterprise.

Mohammed Mehmet was Director of Children's Services in Peterborough at the time this particular building programme was being commissioned. He is clear about the lessons that he learned to inform similar projects in future. He picks out three in particular:

> **Think wider earlier** The link among school building, local regeneration agendas and locality planning around Children's Services is important and easy to miss if it is not considered right from the earliest stage of preliminary thinking.
> **Never underestimate the capacity issues** It is crucial, both at school and local authority levels, to ensure that there is sufficient capacity to project manage this scale of activity, and this includes access to the right financial, legal and technical support. Getting any of that wrong at the start will prove very costly.
> **Take a harder line earlier on in negotiations** It is important to be negotiating detail when there is still more than one potential bidder for the work in the frame. Once a contract has been awarded, this becomes much more difficult.

22 The 3C challenge – it's what happens inside that really counts

The 'WOW' factor in a new building is very important. Henry Morris secured the services of world-leading architects, such as Walter Gropius, to try to ensure his village colleges were inspirational buildings. The environment a building creates can be a powerful factor in inspiring the community. It affects how students feel about themselves and the way they are valued. It can change the way people behave.

But putting up the most inspiring new buildings, however state of the art they may be, will not achieve lasting effect unless what happens in them also changes. New schools, however inspiring, which simply replicate old behaviours, will fail just as surely as old schools with those behaviours have struggled, because of the way they will be perceived to be irrelevant to, and disconnected from, the real world, islands barely connected to the mainland.

But it also follows that schools which do not have the newest buildings, but which think carefully about the ambience and feel of the environment they choose to create, can still have a profound effect. Such schools challenge historical assumptions about how they work, and are prepared to think through rigorously what effective teaching and learning for the twenty-first century looks like, on the basis of making the learner the central focus of all organization.

In particular, both old- and new-build schools need to think differently, but in an integrated and holistic way, around three interconnected 'C's – their campus, their community and their curriculum.

Each of these 'C's also links directly with one of the five threads of change. Campus relates directly to the ethos and culture thread. Community is about building social capital. Curriculum connects to promotion of learning. All three components and their related threads need to be central considerations in any strategy for building or rebuilding. Taken together, they remind us that it's changing what happens inside that makes the real difference with any school building.

23

The first C – campus (The ethos and culture thread)

Schools are only open to young people for the equivalent of 9 minutes in every hour, as Tom Wylie, at the time the Chief Executive of National Youth Agency (NYA), pointed out recently to the Parliamentary Select Committee on Education and Skills. There is a strong economic argument for schools, which are both a costly resource in terms of plant and a major social institution within every community to be open. Wylie went on:

> (Schools need to) . . . take advantage of the other 51 minutes in the hour and show respect for communities young people inhabit, and their multiple identities (in addition to being school students).[49]

The challenge presented here is for schools to be open in both their outlook and their physical building, but at the same time avoid the limitations of a Phase 2 dual-use model.

Oakgrove School in Milton Keynes provides an interesting perspective in developing our understanding of what this means and the challenges it poses. This is because Oakgrove was built to serve a completely new community, which in many ways its existence preceded. The school therefore paved the way for, and as a result could help to shape, the community it was to serve through the ethos and culture it established.

The new Oakgrove Millennium Community was conceived and built as a flagship project for Milton Keynes in central England. This area of Milton Keynes is a 64-hectare brownfield site on the eastern side of the city. English Partnerships is working with Milton Keynes Council, the South East of England Development Agency (SEEDA), and the local community, to develop this to accommodate up to 2,000 dwellings, of which 30 per cent will be affordable housing. It is intended to be a truly modern neighbourhood, a cutting-edge broadband-enabled community, with all homes, shops and schools linked by a high-speed network. Plans for the Community also include a visitor centre, a multi-purpose health centre, shops, a nursery, a commercial centre and a landscaped wildlife corridor. Amidst all this, the secondary school has a key role to play because of its size and significance.

The new school's building is unusual and received recent European recognition. It is one of the most environmentally advanced in the country. It is the first secondary school built to the BREEAM (Building Research Establishment Environmental Assessment Method) 'Excellent' standard, using sustainable materials, and with numerous energy-saving features, such as solar and geothermal power, rainwater harvesting and automatic lighting. The 'green' agenda is also reflected in the curriculum, where regular 'shuffle days', in which the normal timetable is set aside, are devoted to environmental issues. The school also runs an extracurricular Green Club. Oakgrove School is distinctive in its commitment to sustainability, and this permeates its values, its buildings, its curriculum and its catchment.

The school opened in September 2005 with 300 students on roll, growing to its full size of 1,500 students, aged 11–19 years, by 2010. The building programme has been undertaken in three phases with the third and largest phase completed in September 2007.

The school's mission, encapsulated in the motto of 'Excellence, Innovation, Respect', permeates every facet of school life. The blend of tradition and innovation has been designed to respond to parental expectations and values as to what they want from a school, while also setting down some clear markers that the school is also about more than that.

It aims to be a centre of exceptional achievement for all students, combining modern styles of learning with a traditional emphasis on respect and courtesy. Its aims and values underpin every aspect of its work, and, on entering Oakgrove School, students are expected to immediately feel part of an inclusive learning environment, where they will be equipped with the transferable skills to become lifelong learners.

In September 2006, the school received its first OFSTED inspection, which described it as 'a good school with outstanding features'. Its leadership and management, capacity to improve and self-evaluation were all judged to be outstanding.

Peter Barnes, the school's first headteacher, had to face some significant questions in trying to develop this new school for a community which did not yet exist. It was necessary to try to anticipate their need, based on what was known for instance about the planned housing profile, and to seek to develop a match between the values of the school and the community's values as these came into clearer focus.

He pursued this initially through visiting the local primary schools, which had opened a year earlier, talking to children, talking to their parents and talking to staff. Some decisions flowed directly from these exchanges, for instance a decision to adopt a school uniform. Some curriculum decisions flowed from knowledge of the levels pupils were working at in primary schools, a focus on literacy and the adoption of ASDAN[50] qualifications for numbers of students.

But Peter is also clear that community engagement is not simply a matter of finding the lowest common denominator of community wants and then working to that. It is also crucially important to stake out what the school itself stands for and believes. But this then needs to be balanced by genuine listening to people, to understand and respond to what they say. There is a balance to be struck, but there are some values that are non-negotiable.

Listening, and making sure people know they are being listened to, even if their view does not carry the day, is vital. But, increasingly, Oakgrove School is clear this is not best done through formal mechanistic structures. These can serve to distort. Peter says:

> The key is approachable and accessible staff. We go to great lengths to recruit and appoint staff with that in mind. We also arrange a huge number of social activities between staff and parents so they have a relationship and trust in each other. We use informal contact to seek views, but also to test them out. We operate a same-day response to any concern or issue a parent raises. We make sure they know who approach and how to do that. Every contact is logged on a database and regularly monitored.

He believes this approach of 'highly structured informality' is more likely to engage people effectively, and enable them to feel a part of the school, than a bureaucracy of formal committees and representation.

> Relationships and trust are the absolute key. We rely on an organic process rather than structures and systems, but we are very particular in making sure these informal contacts happen systematically and grow.

Oakgrove School was built in a number of stages. The first phase was planned and designed before even a governing body or head was in place. The result was a design that was architecturally well developed, but educationally lacking in some important areas. Two key lessons can be drawn. One is the importance of headteacher involvement from the earliest stages of design. This matches the experience of The Voyager School in Peterborough, where a key factor in securing a successful design was the appointment of a headteacher with 2 years to be immersed in the detail of that. The second lesson is the need to make sure that the school's needs in terms of accommodation are met early in a phased development. This includes an understanding that school needs are not neatly packaged in a 9 a.m.–4 p.m. week for 38 weeks of the year, and that there will be particular requirements for certain spaces for particular purposes at particular points in the year.

With a building in place and open, then relationships with parents can take root. This is not about a simplistic customer- or consumer-based model of parental involvement and choice. The nature of regeneration means understanding clearly the role that parents have as co-educators, and actively supporting and encouraging that role.

There are five things any school needs to work on to do this.[51] It involves

- being open and welcoming
- communicating clearly and frequently with parents
- encouraging parents as educators and learners
- responding flexibly to parents needs and circumstances
- giving strength to parental voices in the development of the school

Pershore High School Technology College and Training School has tried over several years to understand and develop its role in this regard. The school is set in rural Worcestershire and provides education for students aged 12–19 years. The school has 1,200 students, and is oversubscribed. The school has had a purpose-built Additional Needs Provision, 'The Hampton Centre', for students on the autistic spectrum and those with moderate learning difficulties.

Assistant Head Jan Stoney has worked with parents throughout her teaching career. She says that:

> I believe that the triangle of co-education, parents, student and school, is the key to enabling students to achieve their potential. As Head of Learning and Behaviour Support at Pershore I liaised with parents and carers regularly. The Special Educational Needs Code of Practice requires regular liaison and reviews with parents to ensure that provision at school meets the needs of students. I also developed with staff The Kick Start social inclusion programme for students who needed to develop their behaviour. This programme relied on the commitment of parents, as well as mentoring and intervention from school and the development of student's self-belief that they can succeed. This interaction with parents raised my awareness that really we are never taught how to be parents. We all learn how to be parents from how our own parents brought us up. Frequently parents asked me what they as parents should do to enable their children to progress and achieve. I explained how I have parented my own children and suggested methods they could use, but it was not my place to tell them what to do. I then decided, with the agreement of headteacher Clive Corbett, to run the 'Surviving Teenagers' workshops and invite professionals into school to talk to parents about parenting skills.

The Parent Network developed as a result over the next 2 years. The aim of that first set of workshops, 'Surviving Teenagers' was to provide parents with signposts to information to enable them to assist their children with their education and the exciting challenges of the teenage years. The workshops were delivered one afternoon a week for 2 hours for 8 weeks. Initial invitations were by phone and letters, then by informal postcards. Each week a secretary took minutes of the session and a portfolio of the workshops was provided to the parents with a certificate of attendance at the final presentation ceremony. The main aim was to make the events as welcoming and informal as possible, with refreshments and a crèche provided.

A second set of workshops, 'Hooked on a Book', followed when parents asked for information on the learning skills students needed at school. These workshops focused on how children learn to read, the learning skills required at school, dyslexia, assessment and appropriate resources. Jan used the local community centre, 'Number 8', for the introductory session. She wanted to provide a neutral venue that was not an educational environment, where parents may feel more comfortable. She also contacted the local middle and first schools and sent out leaflets and posters promoting the workshops.

The workshops were again delivered one afternoon a week for 2 hours for 6 weeks. The same format of refreshments and informal atmosphere was sustained and a number of parents who had attended the first set of workshops joined these sessions. She had met Bill Bryson when he spoke at Malvern Theatres and Michael Morpurgo when he opened the Fete on the island of St Martins, during her holiday on the Isles of Scilly. She told them of her workshops and they were willing to sign copies of their books for her to use as prizes. A raffle ticket was given to each parent when they attended the workshops. These tickets were put in a draw at the Presentation Afternoon and the winners won the signed books. Again parents were provided with a portfolio of the workshops so that they could use this later as a reference.

The Parent Network group of staff were available at Parent Consultation evenings to discuss the workshops and provide details of future sessions. The school website has a Parent Network hyperlink to details of future workshops, staff contact details and online application forms.

Funding from SSAT helped the school to investigate and develop the role of parents as co-educators. As a result, the school identified 'Ten Top Tips' for working with parents as co-educators from the results of the work that was completed over the first 2 years. This work will continue to evolve as the approach is developed in the future.

1. Face to face contact with parents encourages engagement
2. Host initial meetings off the school site in a local venue
3. Use postcards as communication not official letters
4. Include parental articles and photos in school newsletters
5. Make a Parent Network link on the school website
6. Communicate events by email
7. Provide a portfolio of information from network sessions
8. Use rewards from celebrities for joining in parental activities
9. Promote widely in local press, radio and TV
10. Survey parents regularly for their views

24 The second C – community (The building social capital thread)

All the schools captured in this book in terms of their development as regenerating schools have invested heavily in building what Robert Putnam characterized as social capital. This is discussed in more detail in Section 2 (Understand . . .), although many of the schools would probably not have used such language to describe what they were doing. Putnam argues there is a demonstrable link between social capital and academic success; the success of a school is directly correlated with its social and economic environments. For that reason, the capacity of schools in challenging environments to sustain improvement indefinitely has to be questioned. Schooling as a process can only ever achieve a certain level of success without that broader view of the factors that contribute to educational success. Regenerating schools demonstrate success on a range of fronts, including traditional outcomes but not confining themselves to those solely.

Communities can mean different things to different people. Any 'community' in fact usually consists of a number of communities, be they based on ethnicity, gender, age, disability, location or whatever. Each community will have different wants and needs that have to be balanced. Engaging with a community means more than ensuring that everyone is given the opportunity to just comment on the services provided for them or on the school's priorities. This is simply an extension of consumerism into the public sector. Engagement also means involving them in major decisions that will improve their quality of life. This is a two-way process, where schools also benefit from the imagination and energy of local people.

Such interaction enables people to commit themselves to each other. A sense of belonging and the concrete experience of social networks (with the relationships of trust and tolerance this involves) brings real benefits. An ethical understanding, though, also means paying attention to the downsides of networks, and in particular, the extent to which they can be oppressive and narrowing. So a focus on tolerance and the acceptance, if not the celebration, of difference is required. There is thus a place for both bridging and bonding social capital.

Cottenham Village College, just outside Cambridge, shows both. It is a mixed comprehensive school for pupils aged 11–16 years. There are 970 pupils on the roll. The College was described in its 2006 OFSTED inspection report as 'a good school . . . (where) some aspects of provision are outstanding'. These include the care and guidance of students, the progress made by students with learning difficulties and leadership. The inspection reported that the proportion of students eligible for free school meals is lower than the national average. Approximately 9 per cent of students are from minority ethnic groups, and few students have English as an additional language. The proportion of students that have learning difficulties and disabilities is significantly higher than the national average. In total, 206 pupils have special educational needs, and 97 have statements of special educational needs.

A centre for students with special educational needs is a key part of the college. This now caters for 100 young people, with a further 50 students following an alternative curriculum. The student support centre was made possible through the refurbishment and re-equipment of the Youth Centre on the school campus, which allowed the transfer of what was then a much smaller special needs support centre to use this venue during the day, when the centre was frequently unused. The enhanced facility was then also available for youth work in the evenings.

Outside funding provided additional resources, particularly a computerized independent learning system, suitable also for use by adults with basic skill needs, and DJ and music equipment, making possible initially the running of DJ workshops for centre students, which were then opened up to all young people in the college and locality. This programme has now expanded to include music therapy, art, cookery and construction. The centre also provides an opportunity for a residential experience for all young people based on an alternative curriculum.

The staffing structure of the centre is unusual. It is managed directly by the deputy head of the school, who is also the school's special needs coordinator. It has three full-time teachers overall, but a significant number of learning support assistants, some paid as instructors, as well as a small number of additional instructors for classroom and outside activities. Some of these are youth workers.

The most striking feature of this scheme is that it has established such a large centre for youngsters, many of whom are disaffected with school, many coming from other schools rather than Cottenham itself, and placed this right in the heart of a good comprehensive school. Those young people will be around the school during the day, out of school uniform, often going out in minibuses for activities that might be regarded by some as 'treats'. The school has achieved this inclusion of what others might perceive as 'problems', and even 'other peoples' problems', with what appears to have been little or no adverse reaction or complaint from parents, school students, governors or the wider community. That is a genuine tribute to the degree of trust that the school has built up over time with its various stakeholders. It has also not been an accident.

This trust has been cultivated over many years through a style of leadership that emphasizes openness and accessibility. There is a close integration of governance and management, with respective roles clear but linked, and high levels of mutual trust. Governors are constantly in and out of school, at any time and without advance notice.

Effective and continuing communication has been a strong feature in achieving this ethos and shared understanding. In addition, the wider community role of the college has also meant that it is known as a resource for the community, with many local people using it on a weekly basis at all times. They know what it is like and they like what they know.

The senior leadership team believe the profile attached to the work of the support centre through the direct involvement of the deputy head has been a critical factor in its success, ensuring both that it is recognized as having high status within the school and also enabling rapid decision-making and problem solving when needed. The head also takes personal responsibility for work with gifted and talented students. In both these ways the attention of senior management is heavily focused on the needs of individual students and on teaching and learning, giving out powerful messages about the core business of the school.

This is possible because of a small, compact, well-established leadership team, matched by high levels of delegation to other staff, particularly Heads of Year who are expected to take real responsibility for pupil progress. Innovative use of support staff enables teachers to focus on their core work as teachers. It also means a gradual breaking down of the divide between teaching and non-teaching staff. Every member of staff has a role to play in the educational process and is encouraged to do so. Kitchen staff, for instance, also work directly with pupils to help them learn.

The leadership team emphasize a 'can-do' culture as a feature they strive to foster and maintain in the college. If someone has a worthwhile idea, whether staff, parent, student, community member, school leaders instinctively aim to look for ways to try to make it possible.

The development of the centre is also not a solely altruistic venture. It brings mutual benefits back to the school, not just revenue income. For instance, it makes possible an alternative flexible response when problems arise with a pupil. There is a framework and structure which enables pupils to move in and out of mainstream classes where necessary without fuss, bringing benefits to the class teacher, able to get on with their job, to the student, in avoiding direct confrontation, and to the student's peers in terms of minimizing disruption.

It is because of its investment over a long period in building social capital, even though they probably did not think of it in that language at the time, that Cottenham Village College has been able to develop its support for young people with significant difficulties, yet meet so little adverse reaction from its various stakeholders.

The third C – curriculum (The promotion of learning thread)

25

Lipson Community College in Plymouth has a catchment area that extends across most of eastern and central Plymouth. There is a large transient population in rented and bed-sit accommodation as well as several large council estates. Sutton Ward is among the top 15 per cent most deprived wards in England on the Department of Environment, Transport and The Regions (DETR) 2000 Index of Multiple Deprivation.

Although the main focus for Lipson's work is the education of 11–19 year olds, its youngest learner is 3 years and its eldest 91 years. The college feels this gives out an important message to students, as well as better use of its resources. In the space of a short time, Lipson's success, measured in terms of the proportion of students achieving five A*–C grades at GCSE, now places it at the very highest levels when compared with similar schools. The proportion has moved from 20 per cent to over 50 per cent in just a few years.

Yet when Principal Steve Baker arrived in 1995 he found indiscipline, low expectations from pupils and parents, and attitudes from many teachers and the local community that could best be summed up as, 'What can you expect from these children?'. The key to its success has been a willingness to challenge assumptions, including, as time has gone on, its own.

One key trigger was the achievement of specialist school status as a performing arts college. As a result 'theatre' is now at the heart of all they do. The 'theatre paradigm' has been used creatively to shift the mindset of staff and raise expectations. The paradox for the school was that students who were able to produce high-quality work, within a given time frame, and to a given specification, in theatre studies, did not seem to be transferring that capability to other subjects. The college identified the key elements of teaching in drama/theatre studies as: active listening, extensive dialogue, group work and regular rigorous self-evaluation. All four together enabled students to take their learning to a new dimension. So teachers in other subjects were encouraged to learn from that and apply those principles to their own work.

The quest for knowledge about effective learning drove development in the school. Leading national outside experts were drawn in to help with the application of neuroscience to learning. Teachers have, as a result, been able to use up-to-date knowledge about the brain to enhance learning, and have written this into schemes of work. All teachers build in reflection, recall and meta-cognitive strategies, which in turn, for example, leads to an orderly transition between lessons – with, incidentally, no bells ringing to mark the change.

Lipson has understood and achieved within its particular context the key to a successful basis for building a school for the future, even though many of their buildings are far from new, through a strong and clear focus on the centrality of learning, reinforcing through structure and practice both its relevance and its lifelong nature. What Lipson has done is to focus on its curriculum and on the development of profound learning as a central feature of its strategy for regeneration.

26 It's all about profound learning

The one key concept that has underpinned recent changes in the provision of public services in Britain over the last few years has been 'personalization', as we saw in Section 2 (Understand . . .). David Hargreaves' thinking on how schools can personalize learning identified a number of different gateways, ranging from the design of the curriculum to student voice. However, he also collected these into four broader categories concerned with learning, support, structures and leadership.[52] With regard to learning he felt that schools needed to consider the role of student voice, assessment for learning and learning to learn. It is the pulling of all of these elements together that provides the greatest opportunity for profound learning.

Kunskapsskolan in Sweden, featured in Change Study 1, epitomizes schools taking this opportunity. Rarely do you get the opportunity to design a building, a leadership structure and a curriculum to match specific groups of learners. Even in Britain with its current development of academies, the central control of curriculum content and the conditions of service of its staff has provided real limits. Kunskapsskolan have been considering whether to expand their model to other countries. But one of their real concerns is 'How will an inspection framework conditioned by an age-related structure and specific subject content judge our model for learning?'

Some people, including the new conservative government in Sweden, may regard the goal-focused liberal structure of their system as lacking control. Others might see it as an immense degree of trust in teachers and school leaders to personalize the programmes to meet their learners' needs. Kunskapsskolan go further by saying that personalization can only truly take place where the learner is at the centre and can exercise some control over the rate and extent of learning.

Michael Brearley, who works in the area of emotional intelligence in schools, says teachers 'too readily leave their footprints over the learning of young people',[53] by controlling the learning environment and the process by which they are required to achieve the outcome. A system that is focused on outcomes, while relegating to unimportance the process of learning, conditions this type of control and structuring. The National Curriculum introduced in England in the late 1980s specified, for the first time, systematic content and the broad structure of subjects to be studied in primary and secondary education. The structure is epitomized by the front cover of the document with its array of different coloured boxes indicating the range of subjects. Although there was always a range of interconnecting themes, such as personal and social education, and later citizenship, power in the curriculum was vested in the subject silos in each school.

The regenerating school looks beyond this structure to see the underpinning aspects that encourage quality learning experiences. It works with young people to help them identify their preferred learning styles. It gives them opportunities to construct the outcomes of their learning so that they can demonstrate skills, knowledge and values in the way that most reflects that style yet still shows their grasp and confidence in the curriculum theme.

There is much written about learning styles, dimensions of learning and strategies to encourage effective learning. Over the last 20 years the way we teach has been informed by a radical growth in the understanding of way the brain works. Teachers have never had such access to the science behind learning, and the way that not only young people can learn, but how they can increase their intelligence and grow in success. We now know much more about the importance of positive re-enforcement and optimistic approaches.

In their book *Beyond Monet*,[54] Barrie Bennett and Carol Rolheiser advance the principle that effective teaching and learning is not just about the science of learning, but has to be balanced by artistic judgement. They maintain that 'the meaningless and superficial application of any instructional process does not do justice to the process or the learner'. It has to be applied with real understanding, using the teachers' knowledge of the characteristics of the group, the environment they work in, the time of the day, the weather, what they had the lesson before. In other words, they have to deploy the art of teaching as well.

> If we consider all of the existing instructional . . . strategies and content areas as part of the science of teaching, much like the colours of paint are part of the science of painting, then we could argue that simply having an extensive collection of colours on the palette (the science) would not make an artist. There is no guarantee that a teacher who is knowledgeable, has an extensive repertoire of instructional practices, and is kind and caring, will necessarily be an effective teacher . . . .. This pushes the idea that art and science have a common ground – one informs the other. For us teaching is an art informed by both science and an individual's personal experiences over time.

The regenerating school, therefore, has to create a climate where educators not only have knowledge of the science of learning but also have the confidence to apply this creatively.

The formation of the Brook Learning Partnership (Change Study 2) had at its heart improved teaching and learning. The quality of teaching in the original partner school was very low, and learning consequently suffered. Rivington and Blackrod High School on the other hand, through a core team of Advanced Skills Teachers, had consistently driven forward the competence and ability of their teachers in 'learning to learn' and emotional intelligence techniques. This was already available with the formation of the federation and as such was deployed in the new school. However, by innovatively timetabling the school over a 4½-day period, they were able to bring together all staff and learning assistants to embed this approach across all the schools. It is this consistent application to learning that makes the difference and builds confidence in the team of educators.

But Kunskapsskolan have been able to go a step further. They were able to start with the pedagogy of learning and construct their schools around those principles. Most English schools are trying their best to develop 'learning to learn' skills, but do so with a curriculum structure and building that are not designed for the vision they seek. However, there have been some noticeable exceptions, where schools are taking a much more imaginative approach and have begun framing a template for a new curriculum.

The Royal Society of Arts (RSA) has developed a competence-based curriculum called Opening Minds[55] with 135 schools in the UK using this framework by 2007. It sprang from the conviction that young people were being increasingly educated distant from their real needs in the twenty-first century. Some of the competences developed are focused directly on learning, for instance, how well learners have achieved high standards in literacy, numeracy and spatial understanding. And have they, also, learned to enjoy and love learning for its own sake and as part of understanding themselves? Students also develop competences in Citizenship, Relating to People, Managing Situations and in Managing Information. Schools have usually developed this work through a series of units, modules or projects that combine some or all subjects in the curriculum. Typically modules last 6–8 weeks. This was Kunskapsskolan's approach, with each year having a core of maths, English and Swedish, but then five or six thread courses.

But just changing the way the curriculum is organized in this way does not fundamentally alter the quality of learning. The regenerating school takes the opportunity to ensure that learning is at the heart of the programme and their plans allow the flexibility for learners to co-construct the work with them. Giving learners the right to choose the way they want to demonstrate they have learned a particular topic is essential if they are to develop an emotionally intelligent ownership of their own learning. Kunskapsskolan, for instance, offer students a chance to follow a structured way or develop their own pathway drawing on seminars, workshops and resources to achieve that, receiving coaching and mentoring along the way.

England, towards the end of the first decade of the twenty-first century, is going through a significant change of culture in secondary education that reflects this approach. In the first 3 years of the secondary phase, schools are being encouraged to see the curriculum as inter-related threads. In fact, the National Curriculum Discussion document[56] has replaced the cover of the National Curriculum with its blocks of subjects with a series of different coloured streamers weaving between one another, to indicate this more holistic approach. But this will require schools to establish effective planning groups and it involves workforce reform. It is essential that leaders understand the main focus, and can as a result drive a real understanding of the opportunities for personalization.

However, it is within the 14–19 curriculum where the most significant changes are being seen. For many years, schools, not just in the UK but across much of the Western World, have been criticized for not providing learners and workers to universities and industry that have the right attitude and level of skill. In Stockholm for instance, the university is working at the moment with upper secondary schools because they say that they have to repeat so much of the curriculum before they can begin their work. The Leitch Report in the UK outlined how, if the system achieves its targets for education and training by 2010, the country will only have just maintained its present competitive position.

Guy Claxton, Visiting Professor of the Learning Sciences at the University of Bristol Graduate School of Education, was recently asked to write a think piece from the Qualifications and Curriculum Authority about learning for the twenty-first century.[57] He illustrated his point by talking about two young people – Todd, an 18-year-old bricklayer who is frightened of being laid off because he thinks he has no other skill, and Emily an intelligent 15 year old who worries that when she leaves school without its direction and structure she will be lost.

There are two good reasons for reconfiguring 21st century education: economic and personal. The well-rehearsed economic argument says that knowledge is changing so fast that we cannot give young people what they will need to know, because we do not know what it will be. Instead we should be helping them to develop supple and nimble minds, so that they will be able to learn whatever they need to. If we can achieve that, we will have a world-class workforce comprising people who are innovative and resourceful. The personal argument reaches the same conclusion. Many young people are floundering in the face of the complexities and uncertainties of contemporary life: the relatively successful children like Emily, as much as the more conspicuous failures of the education system such as Todd. Emily sees herself as ready for a life of tests, but not the tests of life. Todd does not even believe that he has it in him to master a new skill. They differ greatly in how literate and numerate they are, but Emily and Todd are both, in their different ways, *illearnerate*. They do not think of themselves as effective real-life learners. They think that school has not only failed to give them what they need, it has actually compounded the problem. Many young people live in a *Matrix* world, in which there is often no consensual reality, no agreement about what to do for the best, and in which nobody taught them what to do when they didn't know what to do.

Their culture of 'cool' is, in part, a reaction to their sense of inadequacy and insecurity in the face of real difficulty. Young people want more real-life gumption, more initiative, more stickability, just as prospective employers and anxious governments do. More fundamental even than the concern with literacy and numeracy is the need to protect and develop young people's *learnacy*.

One of the strands of development seeking to meet these needs is the introduction of a new diploma in 14 industry and business sectors such as IT, Engineering, Creative and Media, and Catering and Hospitality. In the past, vocational qualifications have sought to develop validity with industry after their development. The new diploma has been developed initially from the sector itself, with a Diploma Development Partnership leading the work and then bringing it to educationalists to be delivered and assessed. However, counter to most people's expectations, the real focus of this qualification is the development of a wide range of employability skills, personal learning and thinking skills. These are articulated as the development of independent enquirers, creative thinkers, reflective learners, team workers, self-managers and effective participators. The development of these within a work-related context lies at the heart for this new qualification. But the work-related context has to be real, not one imagined by a teacher who has not been into industry or the business world recently, if at all.

Of course, it is possible to develop areas of work that build the skills of a team worker or focus on how to generate creative ideas, but, to be effective, the whole programme has to live this approach. Co-constructing the work with the learners will develop those skills at a generic level. The regenerating school will be able to move away from a traditional timetabled structure and see the importance of developing longer sessions and modules of work. They will have been developing a wider community perspective so as to be able to work with a range of organizations such as colleges, work-based learning providers and businesses themselves. So that all the learning does not take place in a classroom, and there is a shared ownership of the learners and their future progression. They will have the confidence to take a calculated risk to try something different, because they have the learner at their centre, and a comprehensive understanding of their role in the broader work-based community.

In many ways, these broader skills should infuse education at all levels. In some schools they already do. Take Writhlington Business and Enterprise School in Somerset. Here, in all subject areas, enterprise skills such as communication and problem solving, team working and leadership are delivered through the curriculum. However, the really unique feature of the school is the way that every young person has the chance to be a part of an enterprise company. There were seven companies operating in 2007 from 'Brazil, Brasil' that buys and sells ecologically friendly products at a fair price from sole traders in Brazil to the longest established group, Orchids. This has been built up over the last 10 years and is now supplying seedlings raised at the school to retail outlets across the UK. It supports conservation projects across the world in places like Guatemala and Gabon, and in recent years has developed research visits to these countries. It has even won a gold medal at the Chelsea Flower Show in 2006. Imagine the impact on these young people, not just with their knowledge of botany but their personal skills and confidence level. This is life-changing stuff.

What is more, leaders in the school have been able to take this vision and apply it to their newly rebuilt school, due to open in 2010. It will include a Business and Enterprise Centre, with a conference suite, video conferencing, business offices, and a 400-seat theatre and performing arts centre.

So, regenerating schools do not work alone. They seek out partners in and outside education to bring meaning to their learners. In some cases, this may be part of a wider mission. In the York District of Ontario, Canada, a whole community has focused on developing these generic skills. Their project – Character Matters – has developed ways in which every school and every workplace and community can contribute to key characteristics, such as respect, responsibility, honesty, empathy, fairness, initiative, courage, integrity, perseverance and optimism. The policy identifies how in every lesson, in every aspect of learning and organization throughout the schools, and in every part of the province, they can develop these skills or model them for learners.

These wider skills are what school leaders use to shape their curriculum structure for a regenerating school. They may work in a context with severe restrictions about the content of learning, but these leaders are clear that a focus on the skills that young people need to grow with confidence into their adult lives underpins everything they do.

Key to all these successful examples, one word comes through time and time again. It is resilience. Particularly in this rapidly changing environment, particularly when there are so many pressures on young people to make alterative decisions and where the traditional structure of family and community support is missing, giving young people that skill to see a problem through is a key task.

Regenerating schools, therefore, think very hard about how they provide effective mentoring and support – another of Hargreaves' Personalization Gateways. Traditionally, this is provided by a teacher who meets a group of learners from the same year group on a regular basis. Most school leaders know the difference a committed 'form teacher' can make to the well-being of groups of learners. They not only build an optimistic climate but they are also there to support young people who get into difficulty with learning or their social world. Kunskapsskolan would say that this personal tutoring is the most important aspect of their work, even though visitors to their schools often focus on the built environment and the web portal.

Other schools have tried other ways to build up a capacity in this area. Some schools, Lipson and Ladybridge, for instance have developed vertical structures of support, cutting across age groups. This helps capitalize on the capacity of learners to support one another. It brings experience into the group of young people working at different levels and demonstrates pathways to younger learners.

Many schools are using student leaders in a more imaginative way, with peer counsellors trained to support young people who are experiencing bullying, sports leaders who develop coaching skills in others, and at Rivington and Blackrod, Directors of Voice, who through independent groups of students, support school leaders with eight key aspects of school life, ranging from curriculum structure to bullying and pastoral care.

Other ways to develop resilience involve using adults other than teachers, as well as parents. Regenerating schools are always looking for a capacity across their community to support their learners. And, to be blunt, sometimes adults other than teachers are better placed to identify with learners and their social context. Many schools have learning mentors working and intervening with groups of young people. Others have established links with youth services and industrial sponsors.

In summary then, Hargreaves' nine gateways are a useful checklist to help the regenerating school identify its course of action towards a relevant and successful curriculum. A focus on profound learning is crucial. However, the real key is for leaders of such schools to have the skill and confidence to structure the school environment and curriculum so that, whatever institutional constraints the system throws up, learners can develop those generic skills essential for success in this world. For this to happen, the development of effective regular and consistent staff development and reform programmes are of paramount importance.

Bennett and Rolheiser sum this up perfectly:

> Unfortunately the organisations and systems responsible for the initial development and sustaining of teachers' professional growth often unwittingly urge teachers to work against what is in the best interests of students, teachers and society. That folly is observed in low quality professional development that serves to respond to the endless press of multiple innovations. In addition there is a need to respond to the increasing classroom diversity. All of this is nested in a professional culture that provides minimal time for teachers to reflect and connect. The result is that teachers are forced into replacing meaningful action with frenetic activity.

It is one of the roles of real leadership to prevent that happening.

Change Study 4
The Voyager School, Peterborough, England

www.thevoyagerschool.com

Malcolm Groves

IMAGINE being able to spend 2 years in planning and building a state-of-the-art new school for the twenty-first century that reflects a community-oriented mission . . .

The Voyager School is a new school for 1,675 students aged 11–19 years that opened in the north of Peterborough in September 2007. It was one outcome of a controversial review of secondary education in the city, and resulted from a decision to close two other schools. In seeking to develop a new building that can serve as a landmark within the local community and inspire both learners and teachers against a backdrop of anger and suspicion, how do you begin?

The statement of vision for the new school was not produced by professionals but by a lay group of governors meeting fortnightly over a period of about 2 months. Several of the group had no previous experience of school governance or the world of education. But all shared a strong commitment to seeking the best for the young people and communities they knew.

They were asked to take on this role at a relatively late stage in the commissioning process. They were not formally representative, but took what steps they could through networks, and through web-based communication, to try to share information from the outset, and to at least speak with a wide cross section of interests.

The result of their work changed in quite radical ways the official conception of this new school that had been in place up to this point. Their resulting brief to potential builders stated:

The first young people who complete their full education in this new school will leave us in 2014. They will live and work in a world it is even now hard for us to envisage. Many will still be living and working well into the second half of this new century. Their generation will also inherit enormous challenges from ours. Our task therefore is to prepare them for a future we can scarcely begin to imagine. This is the context for our quest for the highest possible standards of achievement.

We therefore want to develop young people with intelligence, courage and leadership, who are able to manage their own learning and their own lives, and to contribute positively to civil society. Our school will have many young people already facing a range of disadvantages in their own lives, and a number with particular learning needs. Our ambitions hold true for each of them.

To achieve this, we know that we need to create a different sort of school that will require a different sort of leadership. We need to re-think the boundaries between education and life. In many respects it means a school must not feel like a school. In the process of developing this vision we will need to question past assumptions, and we will do that with rigour, using the best research and evidence available to us to inform the way forward. All our decisions and organisational arrangements need to be tested against the extent to which they meet needs of our students and succeed in promoting good learning.

We want the school to be actively involved at the heart of its community, multi-faceted as that community is. We have already embarked on the first stages of a strategy to engage with our communities at an early stage. Our partnership with parents as co-educators is vital to us.

We intend within ten years to have a world-class school. We are therefore looking for building which:

- is, as far as possible, future-proof
- displays imagination and agility in its provision of accommodation
- reflects high levels of environmental and aesthetic awareness
- offers a humane and welcoming environment for staff, students, parents and the community.

The statement went on to explore a number of design and organizational features that flowed from this vision:

We propose to have three 'mini-schools' as the key units of organisation. We are keen that these arrangements should facilitate some element of vertical grouping. At the moment we envisage two schools, each comprising half of Years 7–10, and a third school for Years 11–13.

We envisage a home-based integrated curriculum for 50–60% of the time in Years 7–8 and are interested in the 21st century competencies framed by the Royal Society of Arts as providing an underpinning for this. We expect technology, performing arts and sport to still to be taught as specialist subjects. We envisage ten home groups per year group (i.e. 27 students in each).

Flexible accommodation will permit scope for shared teaching across groups of 50–60, as well as small groups as required.

There will be a strong focus on personalised learning, with increasing options through Years 9–10.

As a principle we see the point at which students take external assessment being determined by need/demand, and not age-bound. Each will be taken at the earliest point at which a student feels ready.

We anticipate a flexible day, with the school open 8 a.m.–10 p.m. weekdays and 8 hours a day at weekends. We want an all-day, high quality, varied catering service providing a range of food, prepared on site, and operating throughout.

We anticipate a six period day of 50–60 minutes in blocks of two periods. As a matter of principle we seek to engage students in longer blocks of learning wherever possible. One result will be to seek to minimise large-scale movement around the building. We anticipate a 20-minute 'brunch' and a 30-minute 'lunch' break, taken flexibly with different groups at different times. There will not a set time when everyone stops work.

We aim to become a specialist school. We expect to seek arts college status with a focus on media or performing arts. We expect to have provision for artists in residence and to support the incubation of community and business arts ventures. We hope to have a working TV studio and radio station.

There will be a strong element of work-related learning for all. 20% of the curriculum for Years 9–13 should involve a combination of work placements, extended projects, community action, and wider learning. All curriculum subjects will contribute to this.

We are aware of the central importance of new information and communications technology and will look to the building to exploit this fully. We seek to be a 'connected learning community', able to develop leading edge practice which extends out into the community.

Such an account is not comprehensive, nor is it directly transferable to every situation. But it does lay down some very clear markers of expectation to those trying to interpret its requirements into the specification for a building. In particular, it tries to encourage imagination and flair in design.

The time to develop such a clarity of vision and a shared understanding and ownership is a prerequisite to the creation of a successful building which allows changed learning and teaching to take place inside.

By no means all of those aspirations came to pass with the opening of the completed building, although many did. Some still remain for the future. Stephen Forster was heavily involved in the commissioning side for the local authority. He identifies a number of key lessons from that experience which may serve to help others, faced with a need to commission a new building that can have lasting impact, to achieve aspirations more completely:

1. Ensure that school projects have professional leadership and experienced governor support in place well in advance to identify community and curriculum priorities at an early stage.
2. Develop at the outset an effective partnership between the Local Authority (LA) and school representatives to validate school priorities and agree their strategy, governance and, above all, funding.
3. Format community and curriculum priorities to define objectives and outcomes.
4. Construct an OBC that supports and facilitates (as far as possible) all the agreed priorities for the scheme.
5. Transfer the philosophy and the detailed planning completed by the school and LA representatives rigorously to the ITN.
6. Throughout the process of negotiating with bidders, maintain the agreed priorities and validate each bid against them, so that the selection of a Preferred Bidder does not involve any compromise in these areas.
7. Use any 'Best and Final Offer' phase of procurement to enhance the agreed priorities.
8. In selecting the Preferred Bidder, pay particular attention to arrangements with the FM provider to ensure that there is no conflict with the ethos and priorities established for the school.
9. Monitor the close of contract negotiations and validate each element of the discussions to maintain the agreed school priorities as far as possible. This requires particularly close partnership between the school and the LA, meeting sometimes on a daily basis. Inevitably there will be some compromises, so it is important to check continually as to how much these diminish priorities and the ethos established for the school.
10. Ensure close monitoring of the building and implementation of the contract so that late decisions or compromises are not made that invalidate all the earlier work.

Section 5
Lead . . .

The comparatively stable and predictable world of yesterday, if that's indeed how they felt to those living in it, is being replaced in the here and now by something very different, as we saw in Section 1 (Imagine . . .). Changes, mapped in Section 2 (Understand . . .), such as the growth of the globalized knowledge economy and population change, are creating a flattened world that is at the same time more diverse, interconnected, rapidly changing and unpredictable. Schools cannot be immune from these forces, and need to change too in order to respond to them. But schools can also have a key role to play in shaping a new future, through their approach to civic leadership and community engagement.

C: Leadership has to be seen as a process based on relationships, concerned with higher order issues surrounding the debate about the role of education in society and then translating that debate into effective and equitable strategies.

D: None of the above can happen without a radical rethinking about how individuals learn and therefore how communities learn.

Two of our five threads of change pick up some of these themes of new leadership, the threads of connectivity and empowerment. And each will benefit from a closer examination now as to what they can mean in practice.

28 Dancing together – connectivity in practice

Port Phillip Specialist School (PPSS) in Victoria, Australia, is a government, multi-mode school catering for a diverse population of students aged 2–18 years with special needs. The student population includes children with moderate to severe multiple disabilities, with associated intellectual disability. The school is recognized as a leader in providing educational, health and welfare services to children and their families.[62]

Bella Irlicht took up post as Principal in 1988, at a time when the school was housed in a white-ant infested run-down little house with 20 students, 6 staff and $8,000 AUD in the bank. Through tireless networking and a belief in the motto 'just do it', the school has been transformed from an under-resourced 'needy' school into a thriving school community with innovative teaching and educational programmes and many resources and facilities. Today, the school has a government-funded operating budget of $3.6 million AUD per annum, and has raised well over $6 million AUD in philanthropic and in-kind support to develop the extra services that have made it the first fully serviced school in Australia.

The school is acknowledged as leading the way in integrated service provision. It presents a new and integrated approach to structuring educational, medical, paramedical and mental health services in ways that enhance greatly the available resources and outcomes both for students and the broader community.

PPSS is the only Australian state school with an incorporated Foundation to support its activities and draws on a 'partnership bank' of high-profile personalities, corporate partners and philanthropic foundations, who all commit an enormous amount of energy and resource to the development and maintenance of the school and its services.

Today the school has a total of 151 students and 60 staff, and is the first such school in Australia to feature an Arts-based integrated curriculum to assist the learning and development of children with special needs. This approach is based on the understanding that each student is a unique individual, worthy of unconditional respect and commitment. Because each student has specialist needs, the curriculum is designed to explore how best to help their progress through a range of education, specialist and therapeutic services.

One of the school's major partnerships is with the Pratt Foundation and Victorian State Government to develop a fully serviced performing arts centre with performance space, audio/visual recording studio, arts room and gymnasium. Other partnerships at PPSS with philanthropic support include the following:

- The Pratt Foundation
- The Thiese Independent Living House
- The Nell Griffin Information Technology Centre
- Helen Macpherson Smith Dental Clinic
- The Elaine Paul Paramedical Centre
- The Lady Brockhoff Music Centre
- Josh Sady Honda (Essendon) Multi Sensory Room

PPSS has also developed partnerships with academic institutions, as well as the wider community. Some of these include:

- A partnership through the Australian Research Council, Latrobe University, Victoria University and Fildes Foundation to research brain and visual patterns of children with disabilities.
- A partnership with the Victorian College of Arts (VCA) and the Melbourne Symphony Orchestra to facilitate opportunities where all parties (and PPSS students) can learn from each other and work together to develop a greater understanding of the arts and people with disabilities. Currently, talented students from the VCA are working with children at PPSS to the mutual benefit of both groups of students.
- Establishment of community dental clinic at PPSS in conjunction with Dental Health Services, Victoria.
- In partnership with Invergowrie Foundation, PPSS runs personal development workshops for women to help them 're-invent' themselves. The aim is to help women know who they are in the context of the world, for instance after raising a child with a disability or the loss of a partner.

From the beginning, the concept of a Fully Serviced School has guided the growth and direction of the school. Today, for example, the upstairs area comprises a dental clinic, a paramedical centre and an IT centre, as well as extra classrooms. As a government school, PPSS is primarily funded for basic day-to-day operational costs. There would be none of the so-called 'extras' (services and resources beyond the government model) were it not for the way in which partnerships have been developed with other government, corporate, community and individual entities. Bella writes:

> In the case of Port Phillip Specialist School, our students are drawn from the lowest 2% of the intellectual community. While that pulls at heartstrings, people in general don't understand why it is necessary to educate children with multiple disabilities. Our partners understand that the outcome of this is that it relieves a burden on families and the welfare system but, most importantly, it greatly

enhances the life of all students and, for some, it results in them being able to make a fulfilling and valuable contribution to society in their adult lives.

By applying the basic principles of running a good business, and making government, corporate and welfare sectors aware of their social responsibility to children with special needs, this school, with visionary leadership, has improved the educational opportunities and environment for its students and set a national and international benchmark.

To make this happen, Bella has ensured over a period of years that the school developed partnerships with a wide range of stakeholders, teachers, parents, government, philanthropic organizations, businesses and individuals willing to lend support. This has taken strong networking, and it has taken time. It is grounded in a clear understanding that networks are not ends in themselves, but must be assessed, as Fullan again notes, 'in terms of changing the culture of schools'.

Bella has always been committed to the need for strong ongoing relationships between 'external' support groups and the internal school teams. But the process of enlisting such diverse support has also not been without problems. Self-interest can sometimes outweigh philanthropic interest. There has accordingly been an emphasis on 'balancing' partnerships – the principle of reciprocity. Genuine partnership requires all involved to be both givers and receivers. And it was recognized from the outset that accountability must be embedded into the process.

All of these point to the need for leaders to be able to manage change in ways which deal with these issues. And it throws into the spotlight the nexus among development, empowerment and management. Throughout, Bella has been strongly aware of the importance of having the big picture, while at the same time aiming for a sense of balance. It is, needless to say, a difficult process, but as Brian Caldwell observes: 'The social capital at Port Philip Specialist School is impressive by any standards'.[63] Brian has also gone on to develop a self-assessment checklist to help other schools identify their priorities in building social capital through effective partnership and connectivity as shown in Figure 10.

What is distinctive about Port Philip is the range and depth and effectiveness of the partnerships it has created. This is what Drew Mackie might call real 'dancing together'.[64] At Port Philip, partnership is a deep and transformative commitment.

But this experience also points to another challenge for new leadership that is operating in such a multi-faceted context. Joe Murphy put it like this:

Leaders must learn to lead not from the apex of the organizational pyramid but from the centre of the web of personal relationships.[65]

So to be effective as leaders in a community regeneration environment, school leaders need to deploy a much wider range of influencing strategies and to operate in a much more permeable, even ambiguous, environment. The new paradigm of leadership places much more emphasis on influence rather than power, on process rather than position. Relationships are key.

The following questions may help a school identify priorities in building a profile of its social capital:

1. Which individuals, organisations, agencies and institutions in the public and private sectors, in education and other fields, including business and industry, philanthropy and social entrepreneurship, would be included in a mapping of current partnerships of a kind that generate resources to support the school? Resources are defined broadly to include money, expertise, information, technology, facilities, and goodwill. What is the total value, expressed in monetary terms, of this support? It is acknowledged that reasonable judgements rather than objective measures will be involved in this determination.
2. Has there been a systematic mapping of resource needs in areas of priority in learning and teaching and the support of learning and teaching? Has there been a parallel mapping of resources in the wider community that can help meet these needs? Have links been made with individuals and organisations that can help identify and mobilise support? Has a plan for gaining that support been prepared?
3. Does the school draw from and contribute to networks to share knowledge, address problems and pool resources?
4. Have partnerships been developed to the extent that each entity gains from the arrangement? Does the school assist each of its partners to measure outcomes, achieve transparency, improve accountability, and gain recognition for its efforts? Are partnerships sustained?
5. Is there leadership of these efforts in the school? Have resources been committed and have roles and responsibilities been determined, where leadership is distributed?
6. Does the school and the networks of which it is a part receive support at the system level to assist in efforts to build social capital? Is there appreciation at the central level that it is but one of several agencies of support for schools and networks of schools, and that its chief role in the years ahead is to ensure that this support is of the highest standard?
7. Is the school co-located with other services in the community and are these services utilised in support of the school? Such services include health, sport, arts, knowledge, health, welfare, law, religious. If co-location does not exist, have plans been made at the system level for initiatives in the future that reflect a whole-of-government or whole-of-community approach?

Figure 10   A protocol for building the profile of the social capital of a school.
Source: Brian Caldwell Alignment SSAT 2007.

29 Emotional power and leadership

Understanding the power of emotional intelligence is one response to this new perception of leadership. One key tool that can help school leaders and others harness the power of their own emotional intelligence is a measure developed from the work of Reuven Bar-On, EQ-i.[66] This was the first scientifically validated instrument that sought to assess emotional power.

The Bar-On EQ-i represents an array of 15 non-cognitive skills and abilities, organized into three groupings – to do with reflecting, relating and responding. Its primary purpose is to improve personal resilience and performance by learning to become more conscious of emotional intentions, the underlying predispositions each of us has to an emotional response, which then influence our thinking and behaviour, and, through that awareness, to enable us to become more skilful in understanding and working with emotional power.

One of the advantages of this model is that whereas the more common concept of 'emotional intelligence' conveys an impression of a fixed factor or element, and carries connotations of better/worse or higher/lower, the notion of emotional power is more neutral and not constrained in the same way. It can be developed and trained, a bit like an athlete's muscles perhaps.

A programme such as EQ-i can provide school leaders with insight into which particular approaches are likely to be effective in working with which groups. Leaders with different professional backgrounds working in other agencies bring with them distinctive value sets that do not always resonate well with education leaders. EQ-i enables participants to gauge the profiles of other stakeholders and inform their strategic choices. Part of the EQ-i Emotional Power toolkit is an approach to problem solving known as Action Tracks. This is a means of quality assuring one's own thinking so as to ensure that all possible angles have been considered when contemplating a complex or frustrating issue.

The EQ-i toolkit has been used as an integral part of the SSAT Community Leadership Programme. Participants frequently commented on the difficulties they encounter when working for a significant length of time with stakeholders beyond the school boundaries.

'They don't share the same values as we have'.

'They have different professional backgrounds from us'.

'They don't seem to have the same ethos as us'.

are typical of some of the comments voiced. One of the traits measured by the EQ-i is a predisposition referred to as Interpersonal Relations. This is about the participant's propensity to cultivate close, friendly relationships with stakeholders and other professionals. One of the more surprising findings to emerge from early school leader groups working with EQ-i was the comparatively low scores achieved in this area. There was a tendency to regard this as a failing on the part of the third parties. Taking responsibility for one's own behaviour was not seen as a necessary step.

By contrast, one of the highest scoring traits was Independence, which addresses the degree to which an individual is predisposed to have an autonomous style, pursuing their own agenda, sometimes even at variance with that of the school's leadership team. In extreme cases, this can manifest itself to colleagues as being difficult to manage. For one participant, her high score in this trait provided a key insight; colleagues and managers had frequently told her she was difficult to manage, but without her ever truly understanding the reason for this. But it also gives an insight into the dogged persistence of the 'silo' mentality, to which Mohammed Mehmet referred in Section 2 (Understand . . .), as education, social services and health professionals struggle to refocus to put the needs of the child and young person as the centre of all thinking and decisions, in contrast to the mindset of 'only we understand this'.

30 Empowerment – understanding and applying loose–tight

Leading for regeneration and change requires the emotionally powerful skills and qualities of new leadership. It also means having a depth of understanding about what needs to be held onto tightly, at all costs, and what needs to be held much more loosely to enable others to grow and lead. It is about the linkage of empowerment and core values.

Hugh Howe is now in his third headship of schools in challenging circumstances and he reflects on the lessons in leadership this has provided. He knows at first hand how the skills and qualities of new leadership have been put to the test in the last few years in a very profound way.

For him, it is vital for all to understand the whole context in which the school works and operates. Context matters, and so matching this to the appropriate style of leadership is a key factor in bringing about the regeneration and transformation of schools.

Take, for example, his experience of leading a school within the Fresh Start initiative. This UK policy originated in 1997 when the new Labour government was able to articulate a vision and a clear purpose in saying that education was its priority number one, two and three. With such a profound and sharp governmental lead, it was inevitable that those schools, often in challenging inner city areas, with low outturns (low, that is, against national norms, but in some cases appropriate to context of the challenge of the children within them) found themselves under increasing pressure, through the political and educational initiative called 'Fresh Start', which, at both its crudest and its most profound level, clearly stated that a school either needed to improve, or be given a fresh start. This meant new leadership and some new investment, while still working with the same children, the same communities and in most cases the same staff. To fail meant quite bluntly to be closed.

Hugh's experience of leading a Fresh Start school in the North of England, in an area closely linked to the then Education Secretary, David Blunkett, made the context for leadership a real challenge, with a high-stakes profile. The context here was to move forward a school that, for many years, had been deemed to be wanting in aspects of its achievement, especially judged by local and national standards. This included poor discipline, poor achievement or underachievement by students, falling rolls and poor buildings. As a result, the local population shunned the school and travelled huge distances to move out of the catchment area. What was required of leadership in this situation was to be bold, and yet also to return to some traditional values and expectations. Hugh explains:

> One of the things which we were able to do, was to focus on some of the fundamentals and to make those clear. This provided the concept of a recipe for success. Fundamentally it began with leadership within the classroom to re-empower professional colleagues to take hold of teaching and learning to ensure the children made progress within a disciplined and ordered environment. It also meant a clear vision, articulated to the students and staff, and importantly to the wider community, as to where the school would be going. Not today, not tomorrow, but in the medium to long term. And it then meant taking clear, tangible, overt steps towards realising that vision. We needed to have at that stage a clear focus of what it is that we come to school to do. To remind professional colleagues that they are there to teach, with all that implies in planning for success, in being able to motivate children, and to regain the love and the passion that they have for learning, and therefore to translate that and pass it on the next generation.

So the context of leadership is absolutely vital. But in a context such as Fresh Start, or in schools needing to improve urgently as a result of a poor outcome from inspection, the style of leadership is also pivotal. In many ways, a democratic, consultative style, will achieve some aspects of this improvement, but some schools facing deep-rooted challenge require strong leadership, which has clear vision, a focus on learning and teaching, on the establishment of partnerships and a style which may even seem at times dictatorial. Some things will not be up for negotiation, and this can from time to time create tensions within a workforce where consultation, negotiation and empowerment is often seen as the norm in order to achieve successful developments. More autocratic leadership can be required at times in order to drive through and consolidate the change process.

One of the skills for the able leader is to understand the changing point at which the qualities that are needed to bring about transformation, therefore, need to change, and to signal quite clearly, to staff and to others, the style and tone of leadership that empowers them more and brings them more fully into a process of consultation and decision-making.

The argument here is that, while the context may not always change, the style of leadership and the approach to leadership need to be sensitive and relate to the most appropriate way to bring about, and sustain, the change needed. The legacy should be that leadership resides not only in individuals, but also in the culture and ethos that are created, the way of doing things, the style of doing things.

Some of the most successful leaders are able to adapt their style, to match their style to the change in circumstances and contexts in which they work. Others are clear in their own mind that their style and approach is one more of giving outline shape and direction, rather than having the skill and the knowledge to follow through with detailed shaping and then consolidating the regeneration of change.

So leadership is a key ingredient in the recipe for schools to regenerate and to provide the momentum in terms of change. Leaders in this approach are pathfinders, risk-takers and must open themselves to being perpetual learners.

Here's Hugh Howe again

> In finding new pathways to move through the regeneration agenda we have, at times, to cross boundaries, and to harness that to the values and principles to which we hold firm. For example, re-establishing the fact that as a school, we could not and did not exist within a vacuum meant we had to find new ways, working with new sectors, in order to benefit the school. Leaders need at times to take risks. They are not risks with the educational opportunities and futures of young people, but risks in terms of thinking outside of the box, and trying to ensure that the manner in which we work embraces and encourages others to think differently. Risk, for instance, in the appointment of young, dynamic staff, who will require support and yet challenge us by bringing a different perspective to the way in which leadership and management operate within the school. And we have to embrace the concept that as leaders, we too are learners, perpetually learning. Learning about the boundaries that we need to work to, learning about the way in which we can cross those boundaries to find new paths and take risks.

In his book, *From Good to Great*,[67] Jim Collins talks about leadership at Level Five. While this is not set within an education context, there is much that schools can learn. Level Five is described as the highest form of leadership. It is deemed to be absolutely essential during pivotal transition years. It is about moving forward with thirst and ambition for the company. It is where leaders plan for even more success and they do what needs to be done in order to secure and generate the ongoing element of improvement. These leaders are deemed to be self-effacing and somewhat understated. That means it is not they who are the important element, but the qualities of leading and motivating others are at the forefront. They foster within others a quest for sustained results. For it is of no value to a company, especially within a commercial sense, to fall back and rely on just maintaining successes and gains. They will quickly be overtaken. Another important element is that everyone takes full responsibility for aspects of achievement and performance that may not be successful, but without falling into a blame culture. For Hugh Howe this means:

> The ultimate achievement of school improvement, of regenerating the school, is to see a transformation in the culture, and this is often the most challenging aspect. It is not what we see that is

tangible, but the ethos that we establish. The feel, the manner in which we do things, that is the ultimate transformation. It is to change the way that the school feels and operates. That comes from leadership which is also transformational.

Such leadership can be characterized as very strongly loose–tight. It is crystal clear about the things that need to be held onto tightly at all costs, the core values and purpose that cannot change or be compromised. It is equally clear and confident about what needs to be set loose (and when) in order to empower others to take things forward with common purpose and clear sense of direction. There is a close parallel here with the matrix model of community engagement described in Section 3 (Plan . . .). It is sometimes necessary to operate in the red zone (the dark shaded areas in Figure 7), but the test of leadership is how and when it is able to move to incorporate the approaches to leadership implied by the (lighter-shaded) green zone.

31   Students as leaders

Interest in involving students as agents of educational leadership has been very minor until quite recently, the late Jean Rudduck perhaps doing as much as anyone to raise awareness of its importance.[68] Yet this idea is critical to the notion of meaningful learning and to skilling up for an unknown future, a core task of the regenerating school. Recent evidence shows how many of our students have little experience of this. Sefika Mertkan-Ozunlu summarized this in a research paper she prepared to inform development at the new Voyager School in Peterborough.[69]

> Student involvement activities (sometimes termed student voice or even consulting pupils) do not necessarily display a commitment to disperse and distribute leadership processes so as to include students as agents of educational leadership. They embrace various approaches ranging from involving students as a passive source of information to engaging them as initiators and leaders of inquiry. This might involve various approaches, from formal elections and representative structures by which students gain access to formal decision-making through to student leadership practices extending beyond schools to engage with the community. Similarly, commitment to student participation in decision-making does not automatically demonstrate commitment to student leadership training and opportunity for all. Very few schools appear to provide any type of formal leadership training for students.

Reflecting on this background, Sefika went on to develop the following framework to help in designing, implementing and sustaining student leadership development programmes for Voyager.[70] It provides a foundation for strategic planning for student leadership development in this new school, and guides the development by the school of options and strategies for implementation. Her framework is divided into three inter-related clusters: strategy, context and sustainability. Each is explained in more detail below. A systemic approach to building interrelationships among the clusters is critical to success.

Strategy

Effective student leadership development programmes acknowledge that teaching *about* leadership is not enough today. So critical features of strategy include:

- content-rich curricula to teach about leadership.
- process-rich opportunities for every student to experience leadership roles.
- making use of real settings which include, but, importantly, go beyond, school.
- strong bridges to the wider community, including business and the world of work.
- well-articulated and clear objectives to direct experiential learning opportunities.
- targeted training on the skills essential to effectively perform leadership responsibilities. This is particularly important to support experiential learning opportunities.
- reflection on experiential learning.
- mechanisms to share reflection with students, programme developers, school leaders and other key stakeholders.
- focus on seeing and building interrelationships among these elements rather than treating them as separate entities.

Context

Outstanding student leadership development programmes operate within an organizational culture characterized by a genuine interest in student leadership. Features include:

- a strong commitment at senior level to developing leadership capacities in young people.
- a strong faith in the prospect of doing so.
- strong commitment to distribute leadership practices to involve students as agents of educational leadership in issues that matter.
- correlation between the overall mission of the school and the place of the student leadership development programmes in it.
- shared definition of leadership developed through collective critical scrutiny into leadership, informed by a sound knowledge of leadership theories and shared by the whole school community.

Sustainability

Critical features of sustainability are:

- a rigorous capacity-building strategy, including both vertical and lateral elements.
- ongoing collective evaluations of student leadership development programmes to assess how well programmes are achieving their objectives, and how they could be improved.
- effective ongoing dissemination of results to key stakeholders.
- networking within and beyond the school for mutual learning. Such opportunities build organizational capacity to improve practice.

32 Thinking afresh about governance

As the change study of Birchwood Community High School which follows at the end of Section 5 (Lead . . .) shows, the governing body in the English school system can play an absolutely crucial role in a school as the guardians of the vision and the trustees of its future. Without that role the school can become buffeted, and thus inherently unstable, either by the changing winds and whims of national policy, or by the particular predilections of an individual headteacher. To ensure sustainability and long-term commitment, the role of the governing body for the future school therefore needs to reflect its own strong understanding of community engagement.

The English form of school governance is particularly idiosyncratic. Democratic accountability or scrutiny is a common feature of most, if not all, public services, and different services do it in different ways. But school governance is arguably the most radical approach, involving perhaps the largest number of participants and based on twin principles of volunteerism and stakeholder representation. An early definition sees a governing body as 'a body of local people to represent the public interest in the school'.

There are three key roles normally defined for a governing body. They are to do with setting the strategic direction for the school, acting as the school's critical friend and ensuring accountability through monitoring and evaluating the work of the school. The three are inevitably closely interconnected.

For the current, British government governing bodies are still seen as school leaders.

> The aim of the Government is to ensure that all children have the best possible education, tailored to their needs, interests and aptitudes. Governing bodies are central to achieving this aim.[71]

The White Paper, 'Higher Standards, Better Schools for All' said:

> The governing body remains responsible for the strategic leadership of all our schools, whether Academy, Trust or voluntary aided. We see an enhanced role for governors as schools increasingly become more autonomous.[72]

OFSTED, in a 2001 report on how governors in schools in special measures have improved their work, identified the following characteristics of effective governing bodies:[73]

- Governors are clear about the aims of the school, and the values they wish to promote.
- The governing body and all its committees have clear terms of reference, and an inter-related programme of meetings.
- Governors bring a wide range of expertise and experience, and attend meetings regularly.
- The chair of governors gives a clear lead.
- Meetings are chaired well, and efficiently clerked.
- There is a clear school plan, understood by all, which focuses on improving the school.
- Relationships between the governors and the staff are open and honest.
- Governors' training is linked to the school's priorities, and the needs of individual governors.
- Individual governors are clear about their role.
- The school's documentation is systematically reviewed.
- Governors have rigorous systems for monitoring and evaluating the school's work.

So far so good. But many school governors do face major challenges in their work to ensure that the school is run effectively in a way that matches the local context. A 2007 study, by a team from the University of Manchester, published by the Joseph Rowntree Foundation, investigated how English governors meet those challenges where they are most acute, in schools serving disadvantaged areas.[74] This research found that:

- Governing bodies can make a valuable contribution to schools if they have an adequate supply of governors with time, commitment and expertise. However, those circumstances are difficult to create.
- Government guidance expects governors to act as 'critical friends' to head teachers and as strategic leaders of their schools. In practice, governors in the study felt happier offering support rather than challenge, and relied on heads to set a strategic direction for the school.
- Governing bodies faced complex tasks. These demanded time and expertise, which many governors did not have. They were also constrained by external policy frameworks that limited their freedom of action.
- Governors had a strong sense that they were acting in the best interests of the school and its students. However, they could not always articulate those interests clearly, and did not have a detailed vision of 'service quality' on which to base their leadership.

- Membership of governing bodies did not reflect the make-up of parent bodies or local communities.
- In some places, positive steps had been taken by schools to increase the capacity and representativeness of governing bodies. However, more radical changes in school governance may be needed.
- There is confusion about the precise role of governing bodies. The expectations on governors have increased over the years, without any fundamental rethink of what they are for.

The researchers concluded that there needs to be a widespread debate on these issues. There is a lack of clarity over the rationale that underpins the work of governing bodies. Their role can be defined in three, quite different, ways:

- **managerial**, enhancing the efficiency and effectiveness of the school.
- **localizing**, bringing local knowledge to bear on the implementation of national policies and the decision-making of headteachers.
- **democratizing**, representing local people in decisions about the local delivery of education.

But the researchers found problems with all three of these. Many governing bodies lacked the capacity to fulfil a managerial role, and do not in any case see this as their primary function. Most governors felt comfortable with a localizing version of their role, but were unrepresentative of local people, had no real legitimacy as definers and defenders of the common interest, and had limited freedom of action. Unrepresentative governing bodies were in no position to undertake a democratizing role as the voice of local people.

Worse still, these different rationales undermined one another in practice. Governors with managerial skills may not understand well the local context, and vice versa. Likewise, governors who genuinely represent local interests may not accept a consensual definition of the 'common interest' of the school and its students. In the words of one chair of governors quoted:

> You need governors who can contribute, so it's a toss-up, between either governors who are representative of the community of the school population, but also you need governors who can actually pull their weight and get the work done.

The report concludes:

> The problems besetting governing bodies arise in large part because, as the school system has changed radically in recent decades, questions about school governance have been something of an afterthought. There is an opportunity now to ask what sort of governance we want and what we want it for. This is connected to questions about how we define quality in education and who has the right to formulate such definitions, about the sort of democracy we want, and about what democratic participation means in areas where large parts of the population appear alienated from traditional democratic processes. There is an urgent need for a widespread debate on these issues.

Some of these tension and confusion are also evident in the emerging national policy pulls that sometimes appear to reach in competing directions. For instance, 'The Children's Plan 2007' states as follows:

> Smaller governing bodies tend to be more effective and highly skilled. We believe smaller governing bodies can be consistent with the stakeholder model and so we will make governing bodies more effective, beginning by consulting on reducing the size of governing bodies.

David Marriott has posed a number of challenges to such a view.[75] Can a governing body be smaller and yet more representative if the stakeholder principle is to be maintained? At the same time, the government wishes to see all schools develop as extended schools, which poses a different kind of challenge that might contradict a push towards smaller tighter governing groups. A school can be extended in different ways and to different degrees by different providers. Where one or more service providers offer their services to pupils, parents and the local community from the school premises, should they have formal representation on the governing body? If so, should each service be represented? Should the representatives be elected or appointed? As stakeholders, should they be represented by a percentage of the total governing body? And with a new emphasis from OFSTED on pupil voice, is it perhaps a little odd that students have no representation on the board, especially in secondary schools (though some governing bodies use the flexibility of the associate member category to overcome this in part)?

If, however, we assume that accountability remains important, even in a reduced form, then other challenges exist from another policy thrust that is establishing academies and trust schools. For the British government, academies and trust schools are two strands in the diverse range of options designed to deliver real improvements in school attainment. Each is designed to work in different circumstances. The Academies programme is supposed to target those secondary schools with the lowest levels of attainment and in the most deprived communities. As such, government believes they represent a radical solution designed to provide a step-change in education in failing schools.

Academies are publicly funded independent schools. Their independent status allows them the flexibility to be innovative and creative in their curriculum, staffing and governance. Academies, therefore, work in different ways to traditional local authority schools, although it is not entirely clear why local authority schools should be disbarred from being flexible, innovative or creative.

The governing body of an academy is accountable to the Secretary of State through the requirements of a Funding Agreement. The Funding Agreement requires the governing body to publish procedures of its meetings. As charitable companies, academies must also prepare and file annual accounts with the Charity Commission, prepare an annual report for the Charity Commissioners, and ensure that their accounts are independently audited.

According to the DCSF, each academy will be under the control of its governing body, which will have a clearly defined strategic role in shaping the success of the academy:

> The DCSF does not prescribe the numbers of governors on an academy governing body, though it is usual for an academy to have around 13 governors. The Sponsor is able to appoint the majority of governors, typically around seven out of thirteen governors, and this must be agreed with the DCSF. Each academy governing body is also made up of the principal, in an ex-officio capacity, a local authority representative, and at least one elected parent representative. Most academies also have a teacher governor (either elected or appointed), a staff governor (either elected or appointed) and many include community representatives. Where an academy is an extended school, they may consider having representatives from the various joined-up services on the governing body. The governing body can also appoint co-opted governors. All members of an academy governing body are appointed on the basis of the contribution that they will make to the school and have a legal duty to act only in the interest of the academy.

That last phrase about legal duty is particularly interesting in its lack of any wider local or community perspective.

And if we turn to look at the parallel policy of trust schools, we find some similar possible ambiguities. A trust school is legally a foundation school supported by a charitable foundation that appoints a number of its governors. A small number of schools with a foundation already exist under education legislation, but at present the foundation cannot appoint the majority of the governing body. The Education and Inspections Act 2006 puts in place safeguards around forming and acquiring trusts, and enables schools, if they wish, to choose to allow their trust to appoint a majority of the governors.

Parents continue to make up one-third of the governing body, as with all other maintained schools. But if the trust appoints a majority of the governing body there will be fewer *elected* parent governors. Where this is the case, trust schools are required to establish a Parent Council with an advisory/consultative role.

Why would you want a majority of the governors to be appointed by the trust? According to DCSF, a school will benefit from having a majority of governors appointed by its trust because this will really harness the external expertise and energy of their partners. It would also effectively give the trust control over all decisions that fall to the governing body, and allow it to take strategic decisions about the direction of the school. 'This will not be right for every school: it is a decision that each school must make for itself, following consultation', says the Department with apparent equanimity.

So the trust and the governing body remain separate entities. Where a trust appoints governors to a number of schools each school will retain its distinct identity. However, precisely because of this separate nature of the trust and the school governing body, the potential for a duality of governance is significant, with the resulting possibility of either duplication or conflict between the two. It does seem that trust schools could end up with a two-tier system of governance in which, for instance, the appointed governors have superiority over the parent council, or there is an unhelpful duplication of role between the trustees and school governors.

Thus, we have a picture of possible confusion within elements of national policy direction, along with a number of real problems on the ground. The Joseph Rowntree report identified three options for change to address this situation:

- **Incremental improvement**. Governing bodies could remain much as they are, but imaginative practices for widening recruitment and encouraging participation could be adopted more widely. At the same time, the Government could reduce the demands placed on governing bodies and consider more carefully the implications for the work of governors in any future reforms.
- **Structural change**. Other education systems manage without governing bodies. In principle, governors could be replaced by direct control from local authorities, or a government agency set up for the purpose. In practice, they feel, this may be out of tune with the direction of policy in recent years. It might be more feasible to create a core of skilled and committed governors – perhaps paid – to lead groups of schools, with school-specific governors added for particular purposes.
- **Radical alternatives**. The Government is committed to devolving decision-making about public services to local communities. In this context, the democratizing role of governing bodies could be taken seriously. This would mean developing the links among governors, local communities and activist groups. It would also mean giving governors more power to shape the work of their schools to local needs and wishes.

The regenerating school, whether its structure is that of local authority school, trust school or academy, needs to be proactive in giving careful thought to these questions, as it works on the empowerment thread to support a sustainable, secure and owned vision, and consider the balance in its governance arrangements between managerialism, localism and democracy. If not, it could find the ground suddenly cut from under its feet as it seeks to develop a credible and effective community engagement strategy.

33 Redeveloping the workforce

All significant change requires a re-evaluation of the roles and responsibilities of the workforce. This can be about new roles to meet changing needs, but is also about training the existing workforce to step up to the new environment. Few of the situations where educational change takes place are ones where you are starting completely afresh, but rather ones where there are existing staff with clear existing responsibilities, operating in an established industrial agreement over conditions and service. The reason for change may be very clear to leaders and governors, but given the pace of educational change in some countries and its perceived political motivation, many employers and unions approach the alteration with suspicion and cynicism.

Take, for instance, the development of academies in England. As part of an information briefing to members, the National Union of Teachers recently wrote:

> This is the greatest area of concern for NUT members currently working in schools to be replaced by academies and those who will be employed in the future. Academies' independent status means that they have the potential to threaten teachers' job security, salaries and conditions and service. They can operate outside the School Teachers' Pay and Conditions Document. The Government states that it is 'the responsibility of the academy to agree levels of pay and conditions of service with its employees and to employ appropriate staff numbers'.
>
> The Greig City Academy, in Haringey, for example, experimented with a new contract for teachers, requiring them to teach additional lessons per week based on a school year of 1400 hours. The new contract caused significant difficulties for staff and the majority of original teaching staff left. Bexley Business Academy also operates a longer day and it has been reported that teachers are not receiving a proper lunch break. They are given 30 minutes, during which time they have to supervise children. In Bristol teachers had originally been told that their terms and conditions would not change when the school opened as an academy but the Head is now planning to extend the hours the school will open. This is being sold to teachers as an opportunity to work some sort of flexi-time.

At the time of writing, union recognition exists in 11 academies, although not all have signed formal agreements. There is no recognition or collective bargaining machinery in three (Bexley, Walsall and Kings). Conditions of Service for teachers have been hard won, and although the comments above represent the views of one teacher union in one country, they serve to illustrate factors that have to be taken into account by all leaders of change, and reinforce the need to consult widely and engage all stakeholders in the vision.

You might perhaps think that where private involvement in schools is more developed and accepted, for instance in Sweden with their voucher system, there would be less concern or restrictions on the development of new working practices. In fact, the unions in Sweden agreed in the late 1990s to move away from national pay arrangements, devolving responsibilities to the municipalities. This was accompanied by significant salary enhancements and the Government continued to set a minimum salary level. This gave significant flexibilities to the local market, further enhanced by the schools themselves. At Kunskapsskolan, the different working hours and joint preparation time are matched by higher salaries and performance-related pay. There is also flexibility over when individuals can take their holidays and agreed additional work can be paid or given as time in lieu. Despite this flexibility, the unions still meet with the company to discuss conditions, employment statistics and matters of joint interest. The company sees this as an important task. However, they do not have such robust policies as in England for incompetence or capability, and teachers enjoy considerable confidence in their long-term employment situation.

So the conundrum is that in many places the industrial relations landscape can seem to reduce the opportunities for workforce reform, but the regenerating school, with its significant need for different ways of working, must re-create roles and responsibilities if it is to be successful. The reality is that unions and their members have every right to be concerned for the well-being of their members, but that does not mean they are necessarily against all change proposals. Rather they would want to be not just consulted but involved in that reform. So any wholesale change does really require a clear vision and set of principles to be established at the outset. Regenerating schools recognize that achieving their goals will require motivated and committed colleagues at all levels. Staff will need to be convinced that they will receive significant support for training and planning.

It is interesting to note across the change studies in this book that training and staff development often feature as a fundamental part of the learning organization. These schools ensure that their wider regenerative focus is not just an added responsibility for the school but pervades its whole culture. In too many schools seeking to develop a broader community role, either the majority of the senior leadership group assume that the responsibility lies with an individual member of the team, or else the leadership team is committed but the majority of teachers see this as a part of the work of a cadre of non-teaching staff.

That is not to say a regenerating school does not need different expertise. It certainly does, as illustrated again by virtually all of the change studies. In some cases, it also requires specific partnership arrangements or trusts to be established. Establishing and maintaining a broad vision of the community, and taking on board the time required to meet partners outside the school and follow-up opportunities, whilst managing different funding and audit arrangements, requires a new capacity. If teachers, or even the headteacher, seek to take on this role alone, they will inevitably run the risk of failing to meet the core purpose of their school by their absence from it through involvement in a wide range of external conversations and meetings. There has to be a point to a meeting beyond just talking. There have to be outcomes. And if someone without the additional capacity is at this meeting, then chances are that they will have insufficient time to follow up, let alone maintain, the quality of partnership at an individual level.

Rivington and Blackrod High School recognized this early on with the appointment of two key staff to manage the community development of the school and to work in partnership with the other High Schools in the west of the Borough to develop joint 14–19 provision, which takes us back to the issue of the unions. It is unreasonable to simply add additional responsibilities to a person's role without them having any background or experience in the work. If the development of a regenerating school were based on that, it would fail. Even with goodwill and enthusiasm, some staff need protecting from their own ambitions and increasing workload.

So a regenerating school must take a holistic view of the workforce requirements. It is essential that, even in schools that are just starting to move from a traditional schooling model to a more community-focused approach, they take this wide strategic view. It may well be that it all starts with a small-scale development, flowing out of something like specialist school status, or perhaps running a few adult education classes, but as the principles and strategic intent come to fruition, simply allowing the workforce to develop in response to each initiative risks failing to achieve a coherent and best outcome.

For Rivington and Blackrod that opportunity came with the establishment of the Brook Learning Partnership. The school established a business core by appointing executive business and community development managers. The difficulty for most schools in the UK has been that much extended activity has been funded as part of various short-term initiatives. It, therefore, requires a bold and resolute commitment to make such appointments. And yet a failure to appoint risks leaving the broader community mission subject to the vicissitudes of various initiatives outside the school. A core regenerative mission requires core capacity to achieve it. At Brook, those staff have been able to show by their appointment that the investment leads to added benefits for the young people and the broader community.

Apart from leadership capacity, regenerating schools see significant change to the composition of all their staff. All schools in England were recently presented with a significant opportunity to remodel their staff to focus on learning. As part of wide-scale workforce remodelling, teachers were to have a range of administrative tasks removed from their job descriptions. Similarly, teachers with responsibility that was not to do directly with learning were to have those transferred to non-teaching staff. Sadly, the development of extended schooling did not run parallel to this. The opportunity for development of other professionals with a more specific care brief as part of this emerging structure was, therefore, made more challenging.

Nevertheless, schools in England have seen an increase in non-teaching support staff in pastoral, guidance and counselling roles. The number rose from 55,000 in 1996 to 175,000 in 2006. The practice of having a non-teacher heading up a year group of young people, so as to ensure they had the chance to deal with pastoral issues that can take significant time, has been adopted in many schools. The idea that a teacher could do all this outside of their few non-contact hours is after all ludicrously unreasonable. The fact that so many do is testament to the commitment of countless professional teachers.

Here, are just two relatively small examples of how things are beginning to be done differently, working across professional boundaries and drawing a wider range of skills and expertise, with the young person firmly at the centre of thinking and decision-making.

At Gordano School, in Portishead, North Somerset, a new resource base has been created at the heart of the school. In 'The Centre', all of the associated children and young people's support workers are based together. The suite of two offices is managed by a senior leader as Head of Inclusion. Working with him are an attendance officer, a student receptionist, a cashier (part time), the education welfare officer, a youth worker, two learning mentors, two Connexions workers, two parent support advisers and a police Community Support Officer.

There are regular team briefings to review case loads and lead worker responsibilities and strong links with social services, the young offenders team and other extended children's services. Working in a nearby room are two student counsellors and the entire suite is adjacent to the Learning Support Unit and opposite the Alternative Curriculum base.

The second of the two areas forms the Information, Advice and Guidance Centre along with the Examinations and Work Experience offices.

Taken together, this resource has created a nexus for both targeted and universal services within the school, and has allowed students of all ages and abilities to locate a 'one-stop shop' for all of their support requirements.

At Comberton Village College in Cambridge, planned structural arrangements recognize the school, the family, the youth service and external agencies as each playing an important, yet very different, role in how a young person will develop from dependant child into independent adulthood. The work understands that if the different systems within which a young person is located are not working together, the effect can be detrimental to that young person. But when each system works collaboratively and coherently together, then there is a greater opportunity for the young person to feel better able to achieve her or his potential. So the school aims to encourage a collaborative response to a problem, and work with the different systems involved within a systemic family therapy framework. Some problems may be located within the family (as in separation or death of parent) or within the young person (such as bullying or drug-related difficulties).

In practice, the work involves a youth-work trained counsellor, employed jointly by the school and the youth service, working with a young person on their own, or with a family member, or with the whole family. It may also mean working only with the parents as they struggle to come to terms with issues related to adolescence or their own ability to parent.

Heads of Year in the school often suggest individual young people or families they feel need support. Once a referral has been agreed, contact is made with the parents to either obtain written permission for the worker to see the young person or to invite them to attend a meeting with the worker to talk through how they might work together.

In addition to feedback from the family and/or the young person, regular contact with the Heads of Year is vital in tracking changes that may result from involvement with the programme. Changes in behaviour, for good or for ill, may be a useful indicator of how a young person is experiencing this process.

The worker says:

> We start by negotiating what it is we are going to do, how young people might know that a session has been successful, and whether teachers might perceive differences in their behaviour and attitude as a result. We negotiate how long we will meet up for, based on what is going on for an individual young person.

Sessions are based on mutual respect and trust and are non-judgemental yet challenging. Young people are encouraged to understand their ability, and their family's ability, to affect change, and that they can develop the resources and skills to make choices that will benefit themselves and those around them. Parents are helped to look at strategies and ways of managing behaviour and styles of parenting.

Records include details of what goes on in the sessions that offer the possibility for change for the young person and how the young person understood the process. Longer term outcomes are recorded, both from those who have finished taking part and those whose involvement is ongoing. Reviews of individual progress take place on a weekly basis through meetings and updates with key staff. Further review and evaluation of individual young people take place in the Student Support Review Group, which meets twice per term, chaired by a deputy, and includes Connexions workers, the special needs coordinator and Heads of Year.

Young people are able to speak powerfully about the impact the work has on them. They value it very highly.

'It really helped me confront my problem'.
'It's stopped me fighting and being violent'.
'I can control my stress now'.
'It's helped me deal with other people'.
'I've got things out of my system'.
'I've become more open. I can talk to my mother now'.

All of that is a necessary precursor to successful learning and the wider raising of attainment. The one cannot happen without the other. They are interdependent. That is part of what it means to put the young person at the centre of all thinking and planning.

However, here too lies the importance of staff development. Using non-teaching staff in this way assumes knowledge about educational practice, which is not automatic. And it assumes mutual respect and understanding by teachers of different contributions and the way they fit together around the young person.

In addition, at a more practical level, it means recognizing how the conditions of service and the salary levels for such staff vary enormously from teachers, most of whom come from graduate backgrounds and in England have seen significant rises in income as part of the reforms. Asking a non-teaching colleague to take on the work at a lower salary, while seeing teachers' conditions of service improve and maintain a higher salary are bound to cause discussion.

To sum up, the regenerating school must seek to remodel its workforce by taking account of a number of key considerations:

1. Although it is likely that early moves in this direction will lead to the appointment of staff for particular roles, the school bases this on a more wholesale review of needs at all levels.
2. Leadership, in particular, increases the capacity and knowledge within the team and this often requires the appointment of a strategic post of a non-teacher to network and sustain partnership with a range of stakeholders.
3. The strategic intent is shared with the whole workforce and their representatives. Leaders do not just consult but involve them in the process.
4. Leaders ensure that the spirit of the purpose embeds the whole culture of the school and its employees.
5. They are sensitive to the different conditions of service and salary levels of their wider range of employees and value all equally. This sometimes involves a systematic review of responsibilities and salary levels.
6. The school places a very high value on staff development and training, and links this closely to the needs of workforce reform.

Change Study 5
Birchwood Community High School, Warrington, England

Sheila Yates

Sheila Yates was Headteacher of Birchwood Community High School from 1987 to 2006, during which time the school became a successful school at the heart of its New Town community. The school is a specialist Business and Enterprise College, a Training School, the lead school in a Leading Edge Partnership and recently added Vocational Education as a second specialism. Following the school's inspection in March 2006, her leadership was described as 'outstanding and visionary'. Sheila has contributed to a wide range of conferences on many aspects of school leadership and now works as an education leadership consultant.

IMAGINE developing and sustaining a successful community school that is sited in a New Town area, surrounded by three motorways with few community facilities and below-average funding, but which manages to exceed expectations . . .

When the New Town Development Corporation began in the 1980s to build Birchwood, a new township to the east of Warrington in Cheshire, the people who came to live in there were promised a secondary school for their children.

But once the first families had moved into the area it became apparent that Cheshire County Council was reconsidering whether a high school should be built at all.

A small group of parents and borough councillors were outraged and organized a bus to take them to County Hall in Chester to lobby councillors in the council chamber on the day the vote regarding the school was to be taken. The votes were cast, and it was agreed that the school would be built – by one vote! In the process, it was also decided that the school would be built as cheaply as possible, smaller than originally planned and without a sixth form – putting it at an immediate disadvantage to all its neighbouring 11–18 schools. The school was not expected to thrive, professional and political expectations were low.

Fortunately the local community, none of whom were educational professionals, thought otherwise and set about achieving their vision of a successful school at the heart of the community.

In the years since it was built in 1985, Birchwood Community High School has more than fulfilled this dream, and, most importantly, has sustained high levels of attainment and achievement that continue to improve still further. The school is a specialist Business and Enterprise College and, having been designated a high performing secondary school in 2006, was granted a second specialism in Vocational Education. Designated a Beacon School in 2001, it was in the first cohort of the Leading Edge Partnership Programme and is also a Training School. The school is also the focal point for the community's leisure and sporting activities, and includes a joint-use public library.

The Birchwood experience is that it is committed governors who, by appointing the right staff to lead and manage the school, can safeguard the long-term identity and interests of the school and impact positively on the social capital of the wider community.

When Sheila Yates was promoted from Deputy Head to Headteacher in September 1989, the challenge she had, to deliver the vision agreed by the founding governors to build 'a successful school at the heart of the community', looked easier said than done. For some reason, because the school was in a new town area, even education professionals did not have high expectations of the school and, at that stage, the national agenda was not about community schools – which were seen as slightly suspect – but rather about the introduction of a very rigid national curriculum and the development of a target-setting culture and published performance tables.

Over the course of the next 17 years there were several key points when the school's vision and core values were reviewed. Was it still the right vision, or should the school become totally focused on academic achievement to the exclusion of everything else? No one ever talked about 'building social capital' at Birchwood governors' meetings. What they did talk about was treating every child as an individual with talents, and developing 'well-rounded individuals', who achieved their potential but were also confident, flexible young people with a strong sense of responsibility to their community and wider society. As a result there are, for instance, no 'school prefects', but rather elected form delegates and a strong school council, demonstrating a commitment to action learning to ensure that the students understood the importance of equality, consultation and democracy.

There was a time when the demands of the national curriculum threatened to undermine the school's commitment to a broad and balanced curriculum. The Wednesday afternoons that were devoted to enrichment activities, such as community service, leisure interests, work experience, project and coursework, seemed under threat. Once again the governors had the courage to hold fast to their vision and insist the programme was continued. In 2006, 21 years after this programme was set up, an OFSTED inspection praised 'an excellent Extension Studies programme that enriches opportunities for pupils to pursue and develop their interests'. Many current tentative innovations in schools – 'stage, not age', personalized learning, flexible timetable models – are all well established at Birchwood.

The commitment to the school as integral to its community and vice versa is a cornerstone of the school's vision. Under the banner of 'Building Schools for the Future', some fine new schools have recently been built. They are often very attractive buildings that work well as learning centres. But almost all are surrounded by high fences and have sophisticated security systems. What message does that give to the local community or the young people about the kind of society we live in? Schools today are encouraged to be community schools. Both the specialist schools programme and extended services promote community development. But how many sustained opportunities are there for genuine community engagement?

At Birchwood, you will find both the community and school learners in the joint use library and the sports centre – sometimes working together, often just working side by side. Adults going about their daily life provide positive role models for lifelong learning and healthy lifestyles. When young people leave the school at the end of the school day, they interact with the community all the time, and it seems wrong to create an artificial barrier at the school gate. Birchwood takes its responsibilities for safeguarding seriously, but security is unobtrusive and proportional, and the community are always welcome, whether coming to the church based in the school hall on Sundays, attending the monthly business breakfast or any of the many other opportunities for community engagement.

Community engagement has many facets at Birchwood. In addition to the casual, regular interaction described above, adults enrich the curriculum in a wide variety of ways. Over the years local residents, many of them parents and grandparents, have regularly been involved in weekly reading schemes to help those who struggle. The business community provides facilitators for activities in a range of subjects especially in developing entrepreneurial skills and enterprise capabilities. There are mentors to support academic performance and for those needing a friendly, non-judgemental adult in their lives. Imagine the positive impact of a mentor who, on the day of every exam, brought in a bottle of water and a card with a motivational message for her mentee.

There are also many examples of the school out in the community, whether it is the geography department conducting a shopping survey on behalf of the local retail park, the art department providing artwork to display in the head office of an international property company, older learners undertaking weekly work experience in local nurseries, day care centres and primary schools or the music department giving a free concert in the shopping centre. Not all activities take place every year. Needs in the community change and schools have to be flexible, maintaining a commitment to the principle of community engagement while being willing to adapt to the circumstances of the day.

At a strategic level, the school sees itself as a member of the community, a partner in all activities, a key contributor to the area's success as an economic, social, cultural, spiritual and civil society. It is not just a school that happens to be located in a community. The relatively recent national commitment to the development of extended services is very positive, but to be sustainable it has to be totally embedded in the community, part of everyday life. At Birchwood, this means the Headteacher being an active member of the local business forum, and the school having strong links with the town council and other local services, such as the medical centre, the housing association and the police.

This has led to some outstanding partnership projects. Together with the Birchwood Forum the school worked on a project to improve the approach into the area by collaborating on a piece of public art. The forum raised the money and commissioned a sculpture, the school was able to have a series of sculpture master classes with the artist, and the eventual 'Encounter' is a gateway statement that has an aesthetic quality from which the whole community benefits.

In partnership with the town council there is a floodlit basketball court on the school site, used by the school during the day, which is open to the community free of charge out of school hours. Every morning town council staff makes sure that the basketball court and surrounding area are clear and ready in time for the first lesson. The same team also supply and maintain hanging baskets throughout the summer to add to the quality of the environment.

This quality of the environment is also a key aspect of the school's community engagement. If we want the community to use school facilities they have got to compare favourably with the commercial sector. Birchwood is a very mixed socio-economic area but the aim for the school is to make sure that it appears confident and successful. The school believes that if they want young people to have high aspirations, then they have to model being the best they can be in every part of the school, from the staff employed to the building and facilities provided. When the school successfully bid for Lottery money for a joint use sports centre, their pitch was for a centre to rival private health clubs. The resulting building is very successful and still looks good after 10 years.

The original school was built very cheaply due to financial constraints at the time, but even so it remains attractive and inviting, and is maintained to a high standard. Everyone, and especially the estate staff, wants the school to be the best it can be. Careful thought was also given in the original building and in the subsequent extensions not just to having a high-quality learning environment, but also to how use of the building 24/7 could be organized in an efficient and effective way. The key to sustainability lies in the quality of the planning and the commitment in the locality to the school as 'their' school.

Once again the governors play a key role in this and it is important that they include local people with a strong sense of social responsibility. Sponsor governors and professionals with specific skills are very valuable, but they are not a substitute for governors who may not have high-level skills but do have the capacity to rise above the personal and put their community first. Two of the governors at Birchwood, including the Chair, were on the original bus that went to lobby councillors for the school to be built 25 years ago. Although the school has evolved and many of the governors have changed over the years, the vision and values have not.

At the core of the Birchwood model is the concept of a family of schools, which are co-dependent on each other and work together for the benefit of all the families who attend their schools. Thirteen years ago the high school set up an after-school and holiday club for primary children (the first of its kind). The primary children are collected from their school and brought to the high school where they have access to all the facilities. The ICT technical support team and the attendance and welfare officer are shared across the cluster. Senior staff from the high school sit on the governing body of the primary schools and partner special school, one of the primary heads is a governor of Birchwood, and the Headteacher of Birchwood and the principal of the sixth-form college serve on each other's boards. All their futures are intertwined and because that is clearly understood at a strategic level, they plan together collaboratively.

All recruitment literature for the school makes it very clear what kind of school Birchwood is. For the vision to be maintained the staff have to share in it. Every interview is about making sure that the school is right for the candidate as well as the candidate for the school. A key feature is, when everything else is equal, wherever possible the school appoints people who live in the community and therefore have a vested interest in its future success. Workforce reform and the opportunity to recruit individuals with a wider range of skills have made this policy even more significant.

Perhaps the greatest test of leadership is what happens when the leader goes – especially one who has been in post for a long time and is closely identified with the ethos of the organization. Succession planning is not something at which schools are always strong, and yet it is so important. Success built to last relies on much more than an individual, it is about careful planning, ensuring systems which support the ethos are embedded, and that the successor, at all levels, both understands and is committed to the vision. When Sheila Yates stepped down after 17 years in post, the governors' decision to have a period of handover and overlap at headship level (and subsequently for other levels) was far-sighted and helped to secure the school's future.

'Building Schools for the Future' should perhaps be renamed 'Building Schools that Make a Difference in their Communities'. The Birchwood experience confirms that if we want high-performing schools where success is built to last, it is important to create the right conditions for social capital to prosper.

Section 6
Transform . . .

This book began with a challenge – to imagine the impact of a school which consciously and coherently:

- connects schooling directly to real-world experience, including the involvement of a wide range of people sharing their knowledge, ideas and skills, and acting as co-educators.
- contributes to increased social capital, with the school and its community becoming mutual providers of resources, expertise, employment and learning experiences, each to the other.
- makes full use of all that we now know about how humans learn so as to develop profound learning.
- gives increasing responsibility and leadership to young people for the conduct of their lives and learning, supporting their broader development as resilient, creative individuals, active citizens and enterprising workers.

We have seen through a range of examples from different countries how there are schools that are doing just that. As a result, through understanding and applying some key principles, they are bringing about a transformation of standards and services. None of these schools would claim to have the whole answer to the future of schooling and to equipping young people to live in a future we can barely begin to comprehend. But each displays some key ingredients and is creating a recipe for success in their context with their communities. The mix, though, is different in each case, reflecting the particular context of those communities. These schools are discovering that mix through their own well-developed strategy for community engagement.

34 Measuring success

The most important thing these schools have in common is that they are all successful both in terms of the more traditional measures of academic success and in terms of a broader range of outcomes. The two are interlinked. However, that broader success is less sharply defined because we often lack an agreed understanding of what it looks like, and a shared vocabulary by which to describe it.

The success of any regenerating school will be short lived unless that situation changes, unless we can find and gain acceptance for ways to measure this success and to account to the school's various funders and stakeholders for the role it is playing, in terms, which have wide currency.

In trying to do this, it is necessary to seek to hold together a number of competing principles. They are as follows:

- Anything important enough can be measured. We should not be scared of trying to quantify success in relation to community engagement.
- Success, though, needs to focus on what's important, not on what's easy to measure.
- Key performance indicators (KPIs) therefore need to be few in number. It is a mistake to try and measure everything.
- Indicators must be about outcomes, not about intentions or provision.
- This small number of outcome-focused KPIs needs to be chosen so as to create a force field. In other words, they need to pull in different directions. Otherwise human nature, being as it is, will focus on a single target, pull heavily in that direction and as a result distort its real course and destination. One heavily emphasized end is achieved, but at the expense of other equally important ones, because balance is lost.

Perhaps the most useful recent framework that might help regenerating schools begin this task was originally developed in 2007 through the SSAT Community Leadership Programme. It was designed to help specialist schools in England begin to look at their success in terms of their community engagement strategy.

This framework is built around five interlocking dimensions that are seen to be at the core for any school developing its community engagement. Each dimension in the model is first described in terms of an overarching statement or quality descriptor (Figure 11).

EXTENT AND QUALITY OF PARTNERSHIPS	**QUALITY DESCRIPTOR** The school has active, valued and reciprocal involvement in a wide range of networks. All of these are helping to build confident and capable partnerships that use specialism effectively to contribute to long-term and sustainable community development.
INCLUSIVENESS, RANGE AND RESPONSIVENESS OF COMMUNITY OPPORTUNITIES	**QUALITY DESCRIPTOR** The school is widely recognized as taking a leading role in the development of community provision that relates to its specialism(s). It acts as a catalyst for a growing range of community provision. This provision identifies, prioritizes and makes appropriate response to the learning needs of its local communities.
ENHANCEMENT OF LEARNING AND ACHIEVEMENT FOR ALL	**QUALITY DESCRIPTOR** Participants acquire, value and use learning, within the chosen specialism(s), and receive encouragement to progress to further learning.
EFFECTIVENESS AND EFFICIENCY OF ORGANIZATION, LEADERSHIP AND MANAGEMENT	**QUALITY DESCRIPTOR** School structures demonstrate commitment to community engagement. High-quality leadership and governance, defined roles and responsibilities, clearly identified resources and common purposes combine to secure the achievement of planned outcomes, for the greatest benefit of programme participants and partnerships.
CAPACITY FOR FUTURE IMPACT	**QUALITY DESCRIPTOR** There is a clear vision and strategic intent for future development. This is informed by an ongoing and effective community engagement strategy, which builds the capacity both of the school and its communities to support each other for mutual benefit.

Figure 11 The five dimensions of the framework.

Extent and quality of partnerships	⟶ Connectivity
Inclusiveness, range and responsiveness of community opportunities	⟶ Ethos and culture
Enhancement of learning and achievement for all	⟶ Promotion of learning
Effectiveness and efficiency of organization, leadership and management	⟶ Empowerment
Capacity for future impact	⟶ Building social capital

Figure 12 The five interlocking dimensions of performance and the five threads of change.

Importantly, each of these dimensions can also be traced through directly to one of the five threads of change identified in Section 3 of this book (Plan . . .) (see Figure 12). That means they can help a school both to take measured stock of their starting point and also gauge their progress, as it embarks on its change programme for regeneration.

For each dimension, the framework then proposes one core indicator of performance, expressed in terms capable of measurement, as well as two additional indicators, which give a slightly different slant on things. It also suggests some possible sources from which evidence might be drawn to feed into the chosen indicators. It is likely that most schools would need to adapt their data and evidence collection systems to some degree as a result of adopting the framework, but once systems are in place they should not require special extra work.

The framework, which is shown in full in Figure 13, is intended to be a vehicle for annual review, focusing each year on at least one indicator for each dimension. Within any period of 3 years, all core and additional indicators should have received some scrutiny and analysis. The aim has been, as far as possible, to keep the scope and demands of performance review manageable.

The framework is capable of being used by individual schools, but can also be used by a collaborative group of schools sharing a common community strategy. Where this happens, review might focus both on the impact of collaboration in terms of community engagement and also upon the contribution of each member school towards that.

A key feature of using the performance framework lies in exploring the interaction of the five dimensions, not just seeing each as existing in isolation. Each indicator needs to be considered in terms of its relationship with and impact on the others, the force-field effect.

No attempt has been made by SSAT at the current early stage of the development and use of the Framework to identify a range of numbers that might be appropriate to each indicator in order to inform a judgement about a school's successful progress in its community engagement. Each school is expected to ask itself what the numbers it has come up with are saying, and how far they match with what they and their partners expected. Their conclusions will inevitably be grounded in and reflect the context of the school's community. But once more experience is gained in understanding the indicators, it could be possible for schools to use their measurements for the purpose of benchmarking with each other. If that were to happen, it would mark a very significant move forward.

DIMENSION	EXTENT AND QUALITY OF PARTNERSHIPS
QUALITY DESCRIPTOR	The school has active, valued and reciprocal involvement in a wide range of networks. All of these are helping to build confident and capable partnerships that use specialism effectively to contribute to long-term and sustainable community development.

FEATURES OF EXCELLENCE	CORE INDICATORS	TYPICAL SOURCES OF EVIDENCE
A comprehensive range of partnerships is established and active. Each has a clear, shared understanding of purpose, along with agreed protocols and ways of working.	The proportion of partners fully satisfied with the benefits and achievements of partnership working.	• Minutes or other records of partnership meetings • Objective review and evaluation reports of partnership initiatives • Records of mutual monitoring and evaluation of progress • Independent surveys of partner attitudes • Film or photographic evidence of partnership activity
There is objective evidence of reciprocal benefit and value, sustained over time.		
The proactive involvement of the school in partnerships leads to significant outcomes in terms of community benefit.		
The school contributes effectively to local, regional and national specialist networks.		

ADDITIONAL INDICATORS

The number and reach of partnership initiatives generated and sustained as a result of specialism in this period.

The extent to which those beyond the partnership recognize and value the wider community benefit the partnership has achieved.

DIMENSION	INCLUSIVENESS, RANGE AND RESPONSIVENESS OF COMMUNITY OPPORTUNITIES
QUALITY DESCRIPTOR	The school is widely recognized as taking a leading role in the development of community provision that relates to its specialism(s). It acts as a catalyst for a growing range of community provision. This provision identifies, prioritizes and makes appropriate response to the learning needs of its local communities.

FEATURES OF EXCELLENCE	CORE INDICATOR	TYPICAL SOURCES OF EVIDENCE
Effective needs analysis is based on good knowledge and informed by community profiles.		• School documentation and policy statements
Priorities are clearly and openly established, based on wide agreement, and fully reflected in the opportunities available.		• Minutes of governors and other meetings
The opportunities provided are valued by participants, who include a high proportion of target groups.	The proportion of take-up, from each identified target group, participating in planned provision.	• Evidence of needs analysis reports or documents • List of provision and services
Joint planning with the range of partners ensures comprehensive coverage and access. This provision is able to respond to personal and cultural circumstances or needs.		• Registers of attendance • Surveys and other evidence from participants, non-participants and external interest groups
The core elements of extended services are fully met.		• Complaints procedure and analysis

ADDITIONAL INDICATORS

The proportion of participants who are satisfied with the range and quality of opportunities on offer, and the way they are delivered.

The proportion of learning opportunities that have been revised or newly developed in response to evaluation and needs analysis in this period of review.

DIMENSION	ENHANCEMENT OF LEARNING AND ACHIEVEMENT FOR ALL
QUALITY DESCRIPTOR	Participants acquire, value and use learning, within the chosen specialism(s), and receive encouragement to progress to further learning.

FEATURES OF EXCELLENCE	CORE INDICATOR	TYPICAL SOURCES OF EVIDENCE
Participants from the community can demonstrate achievement and learning which they recognize and value, as a result of the school's specialism(s).	The proportion of community learners who have achieved their identified learning goals.	• Analysis of learner feedback, including what skills, knowledge and understanding they have developed
A wide range of community support enhances the learning of school students.		• Exit questionnaires and surveys
All learners, within the school, partner schools and community, develop positive attitudes to learning through the provision made.		• Analysis of individual learning plans
		• Records of accreditation achieved
Each learner has access to appropriate, timely, accurate and impartial information, advice and guidance, to assist them in identifying next steps.		• Records of community contributions to the school curriculum

ADDITIONAL INDICATORS

The proportion of all learners, including targeted groups, who progressed to other learning.

The proportion of school students who have had their learning enhanced through the direct support of community partners.

DIMENSION	EFFECTIVENESS AND EFFICIENCY OF ORGANIZATION, LEADERSHIP AND MANAGEMENT
QUALITY DESCRIPTOR	School structures demonstrate commitment to community engagement. High-quality leadership and governance, defined roles and responsibilities, clearly identified resources and common purposes combine to secure the achievement of planned outcomes, for the greatest benefit of programme participants and partnerships.

FEATURES OF EXCELLENCE	CORE INDICATOR	TYPICAL SOURCES OF EVIDENCE
Clear aims and purposes for the school's community role are shared and understood by all staff, students and governors.

The school development plan and school policies reflect a clearly embedded strategy for the school's whole community engagement with clearly articulated intended outcomes.

Roles and responsibilities for community engagement are clearly defined and integral to the school's structures and leadership at all levels.

The school deploys financial, human and physical resources efficiently to achieve agreed plans. | The extent to which all planned outcomes have been fully achieved. | • School Self-evaluation (SEF)
• School development Plan (SDP)
• School publications
• School policies
• Job descriptions
• Budget and financial records
• Training records and evaluations
• Satisfaction surveys
• Staffing structure
• Senior Leadership Team minutes
• Governor minutes and reports
• Student council minutes
• Staff meeting minutes
• Analysis of outcomes not achieved |

ADDITIONAL INDICATORS

The proportion of staff who identify with the school's community role and who have received training in the last 12 months in relation to its development management or delivery.

The unit cost achieved across the range of provisions.

DIMENSION	CAPACITY FOR FUTURE IMPACT
QUALITY DESCRIPTOR	There is a clear vision and strategic intent for future development. This is informed by an ongoing and effective community engagement strategy, which builds the capacity both of the school and its communities to support each other for mutual benefit.

FEATURES OF EXCELLENCE	CORE INDICATOR	TYPICAL SOURCES OF EVIDENCE
There is evidence of growth over time in the school's ability to engage constructively with its communities, in a way that gives confidence in its capacity to ensure future development with increasing effectiveness.	The extent of involvement of school members and community partners in joint review, future planning and development activity.	• SEF • SDP • Annual community needs analysis • Minutes and records of meetings • Feedback from partners and participants
Structures allow community partners and programme participants to join in full consultation about the nature and development of provision. These opportunities are widely valued and used.		• Budget analysis and projections • Funding applications and outcomes
The school is successful in using its resources and working with partners to leverage further external funding and support for community programmes.		• Strategy for community partnership and engagement (SCAPE)

ADDITIONAL INDICATORS

The proportion of the overall budget for community provision which is generated from external sources of income, beyond the specialist school's contribution.

The value of the other forms of support received from the community for the full range of learning opportunities the school offers, expressed in terms of broad monetary equivalence.

Figure 13 A performance framework for the community dimension of specialist schools (SSAT 2007).
Source: Reproduced with kind permission of the Specialist Schools and Academies Trust.

35 Seven key ingredients in a regeneration mix

Achieving success, and being recognized for that success, is one thing. But it is quite another to know what ingredients need to go into the mix to help make that success happen. The five threads of change described in Section 3 (Plan . . .) provide a narrative which can help mark the journey from here to there, and the SSAT Performance Framework can help to generate some indicators which measure progress made. But what lessons, in addition, can we learn from the experience of our change study schools and others that might help any school make the fastest progress on their chosen road towards successful regeneration? Seven key messages stand out.

Set the controls for the heart of the sun

That is not about self-destruction! Rather it is emphasizing that a school needs to know where it wants to reach and to be heading in the right direction for the really important places it is seeking. So this is about the careful construction of a strong sense of aims, purpose and values that together give an overriding purpose to all that it does. Brent Davies has long encouraged schools to think more strategically, but he defines this process very carefully:

> A strategically focused school is one that is educationally effective in the short term but has a clear framework and processes to translate that core moral purpose and vision into excellent educational provision that is challenging and sustainable in the medium and long term.[76]

He maintains that there are three aspects to strategic development – strategic context, strategic deployment and operational activities. Many schools, particularly in England today, have become too focused on the operational. For some that involves the production of an annual plan. Schools that get into difficulty often fall into this trap. That is because without a clear set of clear values and principles, matched to a rigorous long-term futures perspective, any short-term plan is likely to fail, and any improvement will not be sustainable.

In all of the change studies used in this book, there is a strikingly clear sense of purpose and mission, matched by real passion for its achievement. This essentially moral purpose drives their plans and approach, and it gives power and stamina to their senior leaders. These leaders find the time to develop this sense of purpose. The day-to-day pressure of running schools can result in an excessive focus on the daily routine and its inevitable challenge. Many heads rightly see their visible presence in school as an imperative and key role. But if this is at the expense of visioning, it is misplaced. Leaders of regenerating schools look at the future trends that are likely to affect the school and shape the strategic intent for the medium term to align the school with these changes. The technological changes and opportunities examined in Section 2 (Understand . . .) are a clear example of this. Leaders have to find the time to step out of the present system of schooling and explore new frameworks and approaches in order to know in which direction their sun lies and what meteorites or other threats might lie in their path.

Grow trust like there is a tomorrow

In these successfully regenerating schools, trust has been painstakingly built over time. At times this may have acted as a brake on development. Conflict and tension have had to be faced and managed. But commitment to the values and purpose has not meant their abandonment in the face of initial apparent opposition from stakeholders. They continue to provide direction. But equally they cannot be imposed without understanding and consent.

Communication is vital. These schools use constant communication to help build confidence and trust among stakeholders and to reinforce the values. Every opportunity to help achieve this is taken, and care is taken over, for instance, language to ensure that communication is inclusive and meaningful.

But communication also involves listening. For that reason, all their planning is underpinned by a thorough community engagement strategy. Regenerating schools may be agents of change and may challenge and encourage community action outside the normal parameters, but they also ensure that their work reflects real need, not superficial gloss. They have plenty of hard-earned, highly visible listening wrinkles.

The governing body or board, if there is one, sees itself as actively representative of all its community and takes trouble to see that this is reflected in its composition and outlook. It is clear it is the guardian of the vision and the trustee of the future. A range of other groupings is used to ensure that views can be heard and that there is a wide sense of ownership of the decision-making processes, allied to carefully structured informality. They make a supreme effort to canvas opinion in a formal and informal sense to engage all parts of their communities. They also do not assume that they are there to control or lead on every aspect but can be happy playing a supporting role. In fact, many of the change study schools have taken delight in building capacity in partner organizations.

Leadership is all – and for all

The continual reinforcement of values across the school grows from, and is rooted, in the senior leadership team of the school. If purpose and values are not embedded in the senior team, and if they do not live those ends, it will damage the capacity in the school to effectively achieve those aims. But to be effective they have to be shared. These schools give great autonomy to leaders at all levels to live out their values and principles.

The leadership of the whole senior team is pivotal. The roles defined for each member of the team recognize the broader aspirations of the school. Each has some contribution to make to the regeneration ethos. Michael Fullan, writing about sustaining system leadership, highlights the importance of continually refreshing vision and reminding all partners of the purpose and rationale. Even in schools with the smallest of staff turnover, it is easy to forget those guiding aims that were the original basis of the school's work.

Effective leadership is a whole series of successful events, not a guaranteed formula that is there for all time. It requires a leadership style from the head that emphasizes delegation and empowerment, both of staff and students.

The process of attitude change by staff only rarely happens out of pure altruism. The pressures of the immediate job can be perceived to be too great to allow a wider horizon to come into view. So judicious use of incentives, training and tangible support are also key factors in securing commitment to change and opening awareness of its possibilities.

Finally, there is a consistent, strong commitment to developing meaningful student leadership, consciously developed throughout, with opportunities and experience for all, both within and beyond the school itself.

Strictly go dancing

All schools operate in a complex framework or network of schools and other agencies, often with a local government authority at their heart. They therefore develop their mission to complement, if not always to lead, those broader community engagement and regeneration strategies. Successful regenerating schools ensure that their wider work is a reflection of need and represents real partnership.

The fact that there is a senior leader, who may or may not be a teacher, with a clear brief to know about the community and to know about the school, and to make connections between them is significant. This 'broker' role is critical. Sometimes links will be specific and planned. At other times they necessarily happen by chance. There is, rightly, an element of serendipity, of chance opportunity. But this is only possible because of the detailed underpinning through planned networking and the growing strength of mutual partnerships.

Get real about learning

All the change study schools give students experience of real-world situations and problems, and through that develop pupils' attitudes to lifelong learning. Schools that have no wider sense of purpose other than to meet high standards of achievement as laid down by external policymakers risk failing to meet the needs of young people and equipping them with the challenges of this new century. Regenerating schools do not baulk from a quest for high standards for all their learners, but they see this as a natural outcome of their wider vision not a substitute for it.

There is no common plan in the schools we have studied. In fact, to seek a common solution would miss a key aspect of the development of successful regenerating schools, namely they reflect their own context. Neither is it about just delivering new 'subjects', whether personal learning, thinking skills, citizenship or ICT. These schools provide imaginative curriculum solutions and embody the principles they seek to encourage in the very way they work. If they espouse collaborative learning and teamwork, they live it in the way they work with the community and other schools. If they expect young people to be enterprising and creative, their school must be run in that way.

They look for every way to provide learning personalized for each and every learner. The reader will have noticed numerous varieties and approaches throughout this book, from schools using a web portal to facilitate learning, to schools with collaborative timetables and strong vocational learning opportunities, to the opportunities for distance learning or for students to run their own business. To help make this possible, they make great use of adult role models, parents and workers, as co-educators to help students learn.

There are many other solutions and ideas out there, but regenerating schools clearly link these solutions to a passion for providing a broad, quality and flexible curriculum for every learner. They understand how to make profound learning happen and believe in instilling resilience in the learner to commit to high achievement and ambition for learning well after the compulsory years at school.

Be a place to be

To achieve that impact on the learner, the school needs to be a place that people want to be. So regenerating schools pay enormous attention to the environment they create, whatever buildings are available to them. Every aspect of the building offers an environment of appropriate quality.

The more fluid organizational requirements of their wider role mean that the support infrastructure, including administration, reception, cleaning, maintenance and catering, must all be re-engineered to cope with those different demands.

Not all schools have the privilege of building a new school or see significant remodelling to the same timescale as their wish to become a more community-focused school. However, schools with a clear mission and view of their ideal environment can make significant change and also be in a position to paint a picture for the future that might attract funding. Schools in the change studies have made their futures, and taken irresistible ideas to their community, to authorities and to other potential benefactors, to make this happen.

Get people using the escalators not the staircase

All of these do make tremendous demands on the whole staff in a school. Schools who have embarked on this path have thought carefully about the structures and responsibilities of their teams. They take teachers into new areas of work, for instance, in both a community and a care dimension. They often raise the responsibilities of support staff to become more directly focused towards learning. These schools do not assume that this is a matter of exposing people to the new context and expecting them to achieve the skills and knowledge to be successful through some process of slow accretion of experience. Many ventures fail because they do not appreciate the quality they need to provide immediately by preparing and supporting staff to work in new ways. These schools have therefore embarked on a systematic professional development programme. It is interesting how many of our change studies take on a significant and wide role in training, perhaps as a training school, in order to imbue teachers and support staff with their core regenerative principles.

But this level of change and commitment also demands a more embracing approach to the leadership and management of staff. This can mean the schools develop strong relationships with professional associations and set up systems whereby they can listen to staff concerns. Above all they develop and show a level of emotional intelligence that pervades all their work. They are challenging, but at the same time, open institutions, ready to accept concerns and ideas from every quarter.

36   Now what if . . .?

All seven ingredients in a regeneration mix are at root about putting people first, whether they are learners, staff, parents or community. That is neither an easy thing to do nor something to undertake lightly. Getting engagement right has the capacity to release power and energy within a community and within a school, but that in itself can have unexpected outcomes, as the story of Shotton Hall in Section 3 (Plan . . .) showed.

It is fitting that the last change study in this book comes from South Africa, a country which has seen both such conflict but also the beginning of such regeneration. From that experience, Archbishop Desmond Tutu has highlighted the understanding of Ubuntu as Africa's gift to the world. This almost untranslatable word has been encapsulated in a phrase: 'I am because of who we all are'. It highlights the essential unity of humanity and emphasizes the importance of constantly referring to the principles of empathy, sharing and cooperation in our efforts to resolve our common problems. Tutu explains:

> It is about the essence of being human', 'It embraces hospitality, caring about others, being able to go the extra mile for the sake of others. We believe that a person is a person through another person, that my humanity is caught up, bound up, inextricably, with yours.[77]

The solitary human being is therefore a contradiction in terms. A person with Ubuntu is open and available to others, affirming of others, does not feel threatened that others are able and good; for he or she has a proper self-assurance that comes with knowing that he or she belongs in a greater whole and is diminished when others are humiliated or diminished, or treated as if they were less than who they are. And in that understanding lies the root of regeneration. The solitary school, detached on its island, in reality is a contradiction in terms of its real purpose.

All the schools that have featured in this book, in the change studies and elsewhere, have an intuitive understanding of Ubuntu. They have got it. And they have discovered through their commitment to community engagement, with all its difficulties, uncertainties and messiness, the means to transform the opportunities they provide for their communities and their young people, and to equip those young people with the motivation, skills and attitudes to manage their own learning and their own lives, to participate in civil society, and to grow as leaders with the courage and the intellect to confront some of the most challenging issues the world has faced.

In short, they have discovered the capacity to regenerate themselves and others.

Just imagine, for a moment, if every school were able to do the same . . .

Now, what would it take to make that possible?

Change Study 6
Banareng Primary School, Atteridgeville, South Africa

Bill Temple, Dee Pullen

After a career in schools, Further Education and Training (FET) colleges, and education departments in South Africa, Bill Temple took up consulting, specializing in the management of schools and colleges. He has organized numerous *Teachers' International Professional Development* visits to South Africa for the Specialist Schools and Academies Trust.

Dee Pullen retrained as a preschool teacher after her initial training as a geography teacher. She has worked extensively in the entire ECD field in South Africa, especially in rural areas. Later, as Director of St Mary's DSG Outreach, working intensively in Atteridgeville township schools, Dee was heavily involved in supporting the development of Banareng Primary School from the time Paulina Sethole became principal.

IMAGINE developing a school that becomes a pioneer and a beacon, when most children have not eaten a meal since the last time they came to school . . .

Banareng Primary School is one of many success stories from post-apartheid South Africa. It is the story of a whole-school development programme resulting in a spiral of successes in which the school is continuously transforming itself and its poor community. The origins lie in the self-initiated School Environmental Education Project (SEED), but Banareng's transformation and development are remarkable for its originality, simplicity, processes and, in particular, its effects upon the lives of many impoverished children and their families. Furthermore, since these successes were driven neither by the authorities nor by resources, this story is a tribute to talented, trained, passionate, courageous and supported visionary leadership, responding to the desperate basic needs of the school itself as well as those of its community.

Paulina Sethole became principal of Banareng Primary School in 1998, after coming up through its ranks as teacher and vice-principal. Previously she had taught at rural schools, which probably stood her in good stead for what was to come. Her beaming face and loving hug are an inspiration in themselves to a new visitor. She is the exemplar of leadership that is born out of struggle and the need to achieve as well as to inspire and aspire. Her personal development reflects this: qualifying to teach, as many Black teachers then did before completing a secondary education, she completed matriculation, a Secondary Teachers' Diploma, and Bachelor of Arts and Bachelor of Education degrees through self-study while teaching.

The socio-educational climate following the 1994 new democracy in South Africa was characterized by huge expectations and aspirations for change and, in the terms of the new government's manifesto, for 'a better life for all'. Perhaps nowhere was this felt more than in education, especially in township ('Black') schools and their communities. Quite understandably there were expectations that the gap in provisioning between the more affluent city (mainly 'White' schools) and the township schools would close, with those schools receiving significantly larger budgets to provide good teaching and learning resources and to enable class sizes, which ranged from 50 to 100 pupils at the time, to become manageable.

One of the cornerstones of the new democracy was the democratization of social institutions such as schools. This provided both important challenges and opportunities for school

communities (staff, parents and other local stakeholders) to express themselves and participate fully in decision-making and progress within the school. However, this could not be
taken for granted in a community not accustomed to the responsibilities and challenges of
school leadership, even though 5 years had passed in the new dispensation when Paulina
took over. It was a period of new social, political and education structures, giving rise to
great uncertainty and anxiety among teachers and parents: new school legislation was just
being implemented with an extensive revision of all national policies, culminating in a
new curriculum, called Outcomes-based Education (or OBE for short), that demanded new
pedagogies. Meanwhile, the recently formed Education Departments were not yet in a position to provide the necessary support. Moreover, on becoming Principal, Paulina was faced
with a hostile situation of staff fragmentation, animosity, bitter power struggles and rivalry.

By any standards, Banareng was a depressingly impoverished and dysfunctional school
when Paulina took over the headship. It was a deplorable situation, but no different from
many of the other 27 primary schools in the township: broken windows and doors, huge
class sizes, meagre resources and, instead of decent playing fields, a 'weed-covered, dusty
plot' loaded with rubbish – and of course the 300 malnourished and desperately hungry
children, a large percentage of whom lived in the nearby informal shack settlement, whose
only meal came from an inadequate basic feeding scheme provided by the education
department at the school. In fact, it was everything that is conducive to poor teaching and
learning and to producing disaffected, angry children.

It is against these odds that Paulina took up a positive and determined stance to establish her leadership and credibility to turn the school around. It was fortunate for her at
that time she could draw on the support of various allies, each becoming lasting partners
with the school. It is one of her outstanding leadership qualities that she can see education
in a holistic way, identify key people, exploit opportunities and incorporate them into the
school's improvement programme.

The most fundamental and significant of these support groups was *DSG Outreach*,
a non-governmental organization and a charitable trust of Pretoria's St Mary's Diocesan
School for Girls that had been established to provide support to township schools request-
ing assistance. Through Outreach, she obtained moral support and thorough training in
whole-school development through a 3-year training programme for which the school
signed up. Soon after being appointed Principal, Paulina attended a leadership and fund-
raising training given by Outreach at Sizanani, a Catholic Seminary, where she saw highly
productive raised vegetable beds within brick surrounds and caught the vision for doing
the same at Banareng to grow food for her school children. So her *Feed the Child, Feed the
Nation* project was born. The successful operation of food gardens at the school was to
become the hub of an expanding number of successful projects and initiatives to raise the
standards of health and learning at Banareng and its immediate community.

It was fortunate too that Paulina also enjoyed good support from the parent community from the outset. Once she showed the way with her own first two vegetable patches, they tackled the clearing of the grounds with enthusiasm. In this way, a lasting positive involvement of the parent community as well as the immediate school neighbours began.

A third key supportive factor, and one that was to become not only her lifeline but also of inestimable value to the future of Banareng, was a relationship with BMW. This came about after an official of the provincial education department who ran an environmental project introduced her to Buzz Bezuidenhout at BMW. Paulina accepted his offer of a partnership in one of BMW's SEED programmes to develop sustainable permaculture vegetable gardens such as she had envisioned for Banareng. At the core of Banareng's successful food gardens was the ongoing training and encouragement provided by Buzz. BMW provided very little financial assistance but rather seeds, implements and ongoing training in the science of food gardening and project management. Paulina embraced this do-it-for-yourself philosophy. 'The school must teach the children to catch a fish, not provide them with one', she says. But she goes beyond that, insisting that they also be given the opportunities to know the blessing of giving. So it is that the school has embarked upon its own social responsibility (Outreach) programme to help, for example, develop food gardens at a local old age home and a school for children with disabilities. Also, visitors to the school often come away with a gift of freshly picked vegetables and when Banareng children visit their affluent partner school in the city, they also take something with them. One can imagine the sense of pride and self-worth that this engendered – an educational achievement of a high order.

The food gardens originally came about to provide each child with one good meal per day to enable the children to learn. The antagonistic staff were at first sceptical about the project, but as the food gardens quickly developed and increasing number of people came to visit the school, the staff became part of the school – they became increasingly supportive and the quality of teaching, originally poor, steadily improved.

To understand the dramatic effects on the school and its community and the education the gardens are providing, it will be useful to give some idea about the nature and scope of the food and other gardens.

Vegetables – cabbage, spinach, beetroot, carrots and others – are grown in trenches 6 metres long by 1 metre wide and knee deep. The trench is filled with layers of recyclable waste and soil, beginning with rusted tins, then kitchen garbage of all kinds, ending with topsoil. The children originally collected all these kinds of material from the grounds and then from the township. Done this way, these trenches can be sustained for 5 years.

The trench plot is extended metre by metre to give a plot measuring 8 m × 6 m. Finally, each garden plot is bordered by bricks, which the children have also collected from rubble, thereby cleaning up their environment. 'We can use any throw-outs of the neighbourhood', Paulina says, and the school has become expert at recycling waste in the process. A huge neatly enclosed compost heap appears to preside over the garden plots, which now cover in excess of 3840 m². They produce enough now to feed 700 children daily.

Once the initial food growing plots had proved themselves, Paulina developed a cleverly conceived shrub and flower garden – the Mandela Garden. Circular in design, it hosts a central tree to symbolize Mr Mandela uniting the four main population groups – Blacks, Whites, Coloureds and Asians – each occupying a quadrant, also symbolizing equality, uniqueness and beauty. Next to this is a similar garden, the Mbeki garden symbolizing our advancing history and democracy. These together with the pretty rose garden, other flower gardens and an indigenous garden are used continuously as tools for education in aesthetics, history, mathematics, biology, citizenship and practical skills like brick laying.

The vegetable garden is for the body, the indigenous garden is for the mind

says Paulina and stresses

the importance of aesthetics in addition to food; of feeding their children's spirit not just their stomachs.

The indigenous herb garden is actually used for treating minor ailments. The children plant, weed, water and care for the gardens and large numbers will be seen any day after school doing this. The school has become a major part of their lives, a second home. They learn practically that for the gardens to feed them, they must care for and feed the gardens. Readers might not appreciate that the normally simple act of watering from a hose has not been possible until recently, when a borehole was sunk. Even so, the children have always needed to bring old ('grey') water in bottles from their humble homes to water the vegetable gardens. In this way, they learn the importance and value of water as a scarce resource in a thirsty country. Specific indigenous plants ('weeds' to city folk) at the corners of each plot function as natural herbicides, ensuring the vegetables are organic. Through caring for the gardens they also learn the dignity of labour, that nothing is for nothing and that they can make a contribution for their food in the form of their labour, water and contributions to making compost.

In terms of the partnership with BMW's SEED programme, Banareng followed the SEED Handbook during the project development period. This provides not only a basic specification for the vegetable gardens but also guidelines for project management including seven criteria for monitoring and assessing the project:

- Sustainability: economic, civic/political, social, environmental
- Level of pupil participation
- Level of creativity/initiative
- Social impact
- Level of research
- Project presentation
- Enthusiasm/motivation

Happily, the story does not end with healthier happier children enjoying their gardens. The ever-expanding successes that this project has spawned are equally remarkable. As the project developed it could have taken on a life of its own solely to supply food, but by adopting the above principles and focusing on the school's development, Banareng has been able to incorporate the gardens into the full life of the school, and use them as powerful educational levers and a springboard for all sorts of school–community engagement.

Economically, Banareng has more than managed to keep the vegetable growing sustainable, and even realized profits from the sale of vegetables and flowers to the community (an intriguing example is flowers for funerals and the use of the gardens for funerals). The project has won many awards, some of which have been financial. These profits have been used judiciously for further developments and much needed equipment. A major spin-off has been the donation by the Japanese Embassy of eight classrooms with a bathroom for disabled learners and a modern resource/media centre. Many groups of teachers visiting Banareng under the British Government's *Teachers' International Professional Development* programme have made substantial financial donations, having been both challenged and inspired by their visits.

In the social and civic realms, Banareng maintains close relationships with its education authority as well as universities, schools, embassies, the local municipality and government departments such as Health, Water Affairs, Education, Social Welfare, and Agriculture and Land Affairs. A multitude of overseas visitors have been brought to the school. Some of these departments have also used the school for seminars. Banareng was honoured as an official exhibition site for the World Summit on Sustainable Development, 2002. In that year, Paulina won the coveted Provincial Premier's *Woman of the Year Award* and in 2004 the even more prestigious President's *Teacher of the Year Award*. Such events and visits have naturally attracted a great deal of media attention, which in turn facilitates fund raising and growing the school's sphere of influence among its various local and external communities.

Banareng has become a beacon of hope and inspiration to many other schools in Atteridgeville and beyond. Two prestigious schools in affluent communities in Pretoria have formed partnerships with Banareng to come and learn from the school and provide opportunities to advantaged city children to experience the positive dynamism of Banareng and its township community. In addition, the city primary school brings its children to work alongside Banareng's in the gardens while the high school offers scholarships to promising Banareng pupils.

Other township schools have taken to food gardening with help from Paulina. Her influence has spread across the country, where she has advised on the establishment of food gardens at schools and adjudicated SEED projects in other provinces.

Parental and community involvement and pride cannot be overemphasized in the whole school transformation. What began as clearing the plot continues with the daily preparing of nutritious meals for the children by groups of mothers. Banareng supports its neighbours as part of its Outreach programme, for example providing them with trees for their pavements and gardens as well as training to develop their own food gardens. Neighbouring unemployed men were employed in the building of the media centre and classrooms. Consequently, their pride and sense of ownership of the school have grown. Parents have painted the school, fixed windows, laid paths from donated slabs of disused polished granite; they act as guards of the school at night and weekends and have eliminated vandalism and theft. It is common for these neighbours to come out of their homes to greet groups of visitors arriving at Banareng.

The most important element in the transformation is at the level of pupil participation. The integration of the gardens into the full life and educational experience of the children has been touched on. Professor Hillary Jenks, who has conducted a detailed study of literacy aspects resulting from the project, aptly described this as the 'edible curriculum'.[78] BMW required the school to document every aspect of the project thoroughly. Paulina calls the records she has kept *School Profiles*. The children measure and record rainfall, amounts of recycling material and volumes of water brought to the school, take pictures, make charts, write letters of appreciation to donors, write to pupils in partner schools in the UK and South Australia – to name a few examples. The 'edible curriculum' is ablaze with cross-curricular links. Little wonder then that the gardens have brought such vitality to the educational transformation of the school.

The *School Profiles* chronicle the school–community transformation on an almost day-by-day basis. The various stakeholders in the school are also encouraged to reflect on these regularly to instil a sense of achievement and pride as they see where they came from.

The garden project teaches children that they have the power to transform the spaces in which they live and work, to refuse handouts, to develop skills and knowledge that will enable them to make a contribution to their communities, to understand the relationships [human subjects] with their world. In doing so it constructs them as agents who can transform the corporeal, spatial and material conditions in which they live.[79]

But, finally, and above all:

It's important to have vision, to see challenges not problems, to value your supporters, and not to give up under any circumstances.

Paulina Sethole

Notes

FOREWORD

1. Caldwell, B. J. *Re-imagining Educational Leadership*. Camberwell: ACER Press and London: Sage (2006)

2. Caldwell, B. J. and Spinks, J. M. *Raising the Stakes: From Improvement to Transformation in the Reform of Schools*. London: Routledge (2008)

IMAGINE . . .

3. For more information about this programme, see the SSAT website www.schoolsnetwork.org.uk/community (accessed 2 May 2008)

4. Carr, W. 'Linking Schools with Life'. In *Community Life in a Democracy*. Ed. F. C. Bingham. Chicago: National Congress of Parents and Teachers (1942)

5. The 2003 CBI-Pertemps Employment trends survey shows that 37 per cent of employers are dissatisfied with the attitude of school leavers and 70 per cent with their business awareness.

6. Hopkins, D. *Every School a Great School*. SSAT (2006)

7. Audit Commission, *More Than the Sum*, p. 6 (November 2006)

8. Programme for International Students Assessment Tests (2007)

9. For more information, go to http://shifthappens.wikispaces.com/ (accessed 2 May 2008)

10. Friedman, T. *The World is Flat*. Penguin Books (2006)

11. Quoted by Martin Chilcott, CEO Place Group, in an article for *PPF Education Focus* (September 2006)

12. For more information, go to http://www.grange.derbyshire.sch.uk/home.htm (accessed 2 May 2008)

13. Gunderson, S., Jones, R. and Scanland, K. The Jobs Revolution: Changing How America Works (2004). www.jobsrevolution.com (accessed 2 May 2008)

14. Taylor L.C. et al. *Experiments in Education at Sevenoaks*. Constable Young (1965)

UNDERSTAND . . .

15. The first chapter of this section is based on a paper originally developed by Malcolm Groves for the SSAT Community Leadership Programme.

16. Putnam, R. D. *Bowling Alone: The Collapse and Revival of American Community*. Simon & Schuster (2000)

17. For summary, see Burnham, J. W. and Otero, G. *Educational Leadership and Social Capital*. First published in the Incorporated Association of Registered Teachers of Victoria Seminar Series, August 2004, No.136, and summarized by NCSL in Leading Together to Build Social Capital, National College of School Leadership (2005)

18. Morris, H. The Village College Memorandum (1926)

19. For more information about Sawtry Community College, visit the following websites: www.sawtrycc.com (accessed 2 May 2008), www.multitask.org.uk (accessed 2 May 2008), www.opps-links.org.uk (accessed 2 May 2008)

20. Ree, H. *Educator Extraordinary*. Longman (1973)

21. Quoted by Keeble, R. W. J. Community and Education, NYB (1981)

22. Guidance for the Specialist School Programme, DFES (June 2006)

23. OECD. What Schools for the Future? OECD (2001)

24. Green, H. and Hannon, C. Their Space: Education for a Digital Generation, Demos (March 2007)

25. Salti, R. Reported in *New Scientist* (July 2004)

26. Toffler, A. *Future Shock*. Random House (1970)

27. Stonier, T. *The Wealth of Information*. Thames Methuen (1983)

28. Leitch, Prosperity for All in the Global Economy, HMSO (2006)

29. Friedman, T. *The World is Flat*. Penguin Books (2006)

30. Schooling for Tomorrow: OECD Scenarios – NCSL (2005)

31. Fink, T. *Leadership for Mortals*. Paul Chapman (2005)

32. Daanen, H. and Facer, K. 2020 and Beyond, Futurelab (2007)

33. Leadbeater, C. The Shape of Things to Come: Personalised Learning through Collaboration, DFES (2005). See http://publications.teachernet.gov.uk (accessed 2 May 2008)

34. The Children's Plan: Building Brighter Futures, DSCF (2007). See http://www.dfes.gov.uk/publications/childrensplan (accessed 2 May 2008)

35. For more information, see http://www.arkonline.org/projects/uk_education1/claire.html (accessed 2 May 2008)

36. Beahm, A. *San Francisco Chronicle* (12 February 2007)

PLAN . . .

37. Audit Commission, More than the Sum: Mobilising the Whole Council and Its Partners to Support School Success (November 2006)

38. The concept of the five threads was originally developed for the SSAT Community Leadership Programme.

39. Chanan, G. *Out of the Shadows: Local Community Action in the European Community*. Dublin: European Foundation for the Improvement of Living and Working Conditions (1992)

40. See http://www.partnerships.org.uk/articles/still.htm (accessed 2 May 2008)

41. Arnstein, S. 'A Ladder of Citizen Participation', *Journal of the American Institute of Planners*, 8(3), 217–24 (1969)

42. Wilcox, D. The Guide to Effective Participation, Joseph Rowntree Foundation (1994). See http://www.partnerships.org.uk/part/index.htm

43. Edith Kahn Memorial Lecture 'Civil Renewal: A New Agenda' (1 June 2003)

44. For a fuller account of Karen Stephenson's work, see article by Kleiner A. in *Strategy and Business* (24 November 2006)

45. Karen Stephenson's company website is www.netform.com (accessed 2 May 2008)

46. Gladwell, M. *The Tipping Point: How Little Things can Make a Big Difference*. Little, Brown & Company (2000)

47. Weissbord, M. and Janoff, S. *Future Search: An Action Guide to Finding Common Ground in Organisations and Communities*, Second edition. San Francisco: Berrett-Koehler (2000). See also www.futuresearch.net

48. From an interview for the Specialist Schools and Academies Trust. See also http://seattlepi.nwsource.com/local/174054_ljacobs20.html (accessed 2 May 2008) and http://www.spl.org (accessed 2 May 2008) to find out about Seattle Public Library.

BUILD . . .

49. Select Committee on Education and Skills: Report on Citizenship (2007)

50. For more information about ASDAN accreditation, see http://www.asdan.org.uk/what_we_do.php

51. A useful guide is the booklet *Partners in Learning*, produced by Cambridgeshire County Council, ISBN: 0-902436-56-2 (1999)

52. Hargreaves, D. *Personalising Learning Series 1 and 2*. SSAT (2004–06)

53. Brearley, M. *Emotional Intelligence in the Classroom*. Crown House, ISBN: 9781899836659

54. See http://www.beyondmonet.ca (accessed 2 May 2008)

55. Further information about Opening Minds is available at http://www.rsa.org.uk/newcurriculum/resources.asp (accessed 2 May 2008)

56. See http://curriculum.qca.org.uk/ (accessed 2 May 2008)

57. This paper by Guy Claxton can be downloaded from http://www.qca.org.uk/qca_6141.aspx (accessed 2 May 2008)

LEAD . . .

58. Fullan, M. *Leading in a Culture of Change*. San Francisco: Jossey-Bass (2001)

59. Senge, P. M. *The Fifth Discipline – The Art & Practice of the Learning Organisation*. New York: Currency/Doubleday (1994)

60. Higgs, M. J. Leadership: The Long Line: A View on How Can We Make Sense of Leadership in the 21st Century. Henley Working Paper 02/07, Henley Management College (2002)

61. Hobby, R., Jerome, N. and Gent, D. *Connected Leadership: A Model of Influence for Those without Power*. Hay Group (2005)

62. For more information, see www.portphillip.vic.edu.au (accessed 2 May 2008)

63. Caldwell, B. *Re-imagining the Self-Managing School*. SSAT (2004)

64. http://www.partnerships.org.uk/articles/still.htm (accessed 2 May 2008)

65. Murphy, J. *The Landscape of Leadership Preparation: Reframing the Education of School Administrators*. Sage (1992)

66. More information about the theoretical background can be found at www.reuvenbaron.org (accessed 2 May 2008). The particular development of this used within the Community Leadership Programme draws on the work of Brett Richards and can be found at www.connectiveintelligence.com (accessed 2 May 2008)

67. Collins, J. *From Good to Great: Why Some Companies Make the Leap . . . and Others Don't*. HarperCollins, ISBN: 0066620996 (2001)

68. See for instance, Doddington, C., Flutter, J. and Rudduck, J. 'Taking Their Word for It: Can Listening, and Responding, to Pupils' Views Give New Directions for School Improvement?' *Education* 3–13, 28(3), 46–52 (2000) and Flutter, J. and Rudduck, J. *Consulting Pupils: What's in it for Schools?* London: Routledge Falmer (2004)

69. Mertkan-Ozunlu, S. 'Effective Mechanisms for Establishing Meaningful Student Leadership Programs', Research paper prepared for the Voyager School (2006)

70. Mertkan-Ozunlu, S. and Mullan, J. 'Students as Agents of Educational Leadership: Case Study of a Specialist Media Arts School', paper presented in ECER, Ghent (2007)

71. Governing the School of the Future, DFES (2004)

72. Higher Standards, Better Schools for All, Para 8.34, HMSO (2005)

73. School Governance: Making It Better, OFSTED (2001)

74. Dean, C., Dyson, A., Gallannaugh, F., Howes, A. and Raffo, C. *Schools, Governors and Disadvantage*. Joseph Rowntree Foundation (March 2007)

75. Marriott, D. 'Is There a Future for School Governance?' *School Governor Update* (July 2006)

TRANSFORM . . .

76. Davies, B. *Leading the Strategically Focused School*. Sage (2006)

77. Tutu, D. *No Future without Forgiveness*. Doubleday (2000)

78. Jenks, H. 'Seeding Changes in South Africa: New Literacies, New Subjectivities, New Futures'. In *English Teachers at Work*. Eds Doecke, B., Nixon, H. and Homer, D. (2003)

Index